Sports Illustrated

DEREK JETER

A CELEBRATION OF THE YANKEE CAPTAIN

Derek Jeter floats above
New York in 1999.

DEREK JETER

Jeter at shortstop
at Legends Field in 2001.

THE PHENOM

Chapter 1

THROUGH 1999

Jeter played for the Chandler Diamondbacks in the Arizona Fall League in 1994.

The Yankees hoped Jeter would be their starting shortstop in 1995. A shoulder injury delayed those plans.

Excerpted from SPORTS ILLUSTRATED, May 6, 1996

New York...New York

There's a blast from the past in the Big Apple, where rookie shortstop Rey Ordóñez of the Mets and his Yankees counterpart, Derek Jeter, evoke memories of Pee Wee and the Scooter

BY GERRY CALLAHAN

On Opening Day in a miserably cold mist at Shea Stadium, Mets rookie shortstop Rey Ordóñez went to his knees and brought a lot of New York baseball fans with him. In the seventh inning of a game against the St. Louis Cardinals, Ordóñez scooped up a low throw from leftfielder Bernard Gilkey and relayed it 150 feet to the plate from his knees, cutting down speedy Cardinals shortstop Royce Clayton and leaving eyewitnesses pleading for a replay.

Most New Yorkers come out of the womb convinced that they have seen it all, but Ordóñez, a 23-year-old Cuban defector making his major league debut, left them as wide-eyed and giddy as Canadian tourists in Times Square. It was much more than a spectacular play—it was an original, a wonderfully instinctive move that stood out even in this age of ESPN plays of the day/week/year.

The Mets went on to beat the Cardinals 7–6 that day, and the great Ozzie Smith, who had witnessed Ordóñez's throw from his place in the visitors' dugout, said, "It's safe to say that he's the second coming of me."

Across the Triborough Bridge the Yankees believe that they too have found themselves a purebred shortstop. On Opening Day in Cleveland, 21-year-old Derek Jeter was in the Yankees' starting lineup, the 11th shortstop to start the opener in pinstripes since 1981 and the first rookie to do so since 1962, when Tom Tresh subbed for Tony Kubek, who was in the military. Jeter hit a home run in his second at-bat and made a pretty nifty defensive play himself, pulling down an over-the-shoulder fly in short centerfield to save a run.

Four weeks into his rookie season Jeter was hitting .265 with a .390 on-base percentage. Ordóñez, a weak hitter in the minors who was batting a surprising .342 through Sunday, may be the next Ozzie in the field, but the Yankees

A young Jeter during batting practice at Yankee Stadium.

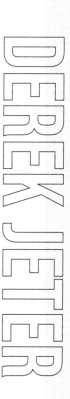

DEREK JETER

are hoping Jeter is a young Ripken or Larkin, an all-around shortstop with a sizzling bat to match his solid glove. "I think patience is the key," says Yankees third baseman Wade Boggs. "But we're in New York. Patience and New York don't always go together."

It has been years since New York has had a shortstop who got people excited, years since Kubek (1957–65) and Bud Harrelson ('65–77) were hits on Broadway for the Yankees and the Mets, respectively. Now the city has two potential stars at shortstop. Now comes the fun part. Now we see if two promising rookies can survive in a baseball town that often eats its young.

Beyond their pinstripes and their position, Ordóñez and Jeter have about as much in common as Havana, Cuba, and Kalamazoo, Mich., their respective hometowns. Jeter is long and lean (6'3", 185 pounds), with the body of an NBA two-guard and the raw athletic ability to play any position. He just happened to choose shortstop. Ordóñez, at 5'9" and 159 pounds, looks like a middleweight fighter, with a compact muscular frame that doesn't carry an ounce of fat. The shortstop position was invented with Rey Ordóñez in mind.

Jeter is friendly and outgoing, and the only time he ducks a question is when he is asked to praise himself. He was proud to get number 2 because all the other single digits (except 6, which belongs to his manager, Joe Torre) were worn by Yankee legends and have been retired. Jeter can match the names of those legends to their retired numbers, a remarkable feat for a big league rookie in this day and age.

Ordóñez is reticent and zealously private, wary of even his colleagues in the Mets' organization. Last year, while traveling with Triple A Norfolk, he was held up at the Canadian border by questions about his immigration status, which didn't help to allay his fear of authority. "Like a lot of Cubans, he's still wary of authority figures," says Mets assistant general manager Steve Phillips. "We're still trying to convince him that we're all in this together: coaches, managers, players, front office."

For now, Rafael Landestoy, a minor league manager in the Mets' organization, is serving as Ordóñez's interpreter. Ordóñez will speak some English to teammates but not to reporters. Phillips says the team is trying to "structure things to make success more likely" for Ordóñez.

"I told him that he has to learn the language," says Landestoy, a native of the Dominican Republic. "I told him that all the sportswriters are going to want to talk to him all the time. But he's afraid. He doesn't want to say the wrong thing."

In a 20-minute interview in mid-April, Ordóñez sat on a stool in front of his locker

"He dominated rookie ball, so we moved him to [Class] A, and he dominated there. We sent him to Double A, and he dominated there. At Columbus it was the same thing. I'm telling you, he could be one of the special ones."

and looked down at the floor. He didn't say the wrong thing or much of anything. "You have to remember where he's coming from," says Phillips. "There was not a lot of trust involved with the Cuban national team."

Jeter is the all-American boy, born in New Jersey and raised in Kalamazoo. As a kid he would return to Jersey in the summers to visit relatives and root for the Yankees. He wore Yankees caps and T-shirts and idolized Dave Winfield. He was a basketball and baseball star in high school and spent one semester at Michigan. He says all the credit for his success belongs to his parents, Dorothy, an accountant, and Charles, a drug-and-alcohol-abuse counselor with a Ph.D. Dorothy is white, Charles is Black, and Derek announces proudly, "No one knows what I am, so I can relate to everyone. I've got all kinds of friends: Black, white, and Spanish."

He is a one-man melting pot, fittingly taking a lead role in New York. As he left Yankee Stadium after a game recently, he stopped on his way to the parking lot and signed autographs for a crowd of kids. Jeter is prepared for the onslaught of autograph gnats and collectibles pests who swarm to highly touted rookies, but he is determined not to let them ruin his days. He recently took an apartment in Manhattan, a rare move for any New York athlete, let alone someone so young. He plans to live alone, even though it makes his mother nervous. In his first season in the city he intends to see more than just his living room and his locker.

Jeter says he has received advice and support from many of his teammates, including one Yankees veteran who knows all too well what it's like to be young and beloved in New York. Dwight Gooden, who broke in with the Mets in 1984 at the age of 19, was twice suspended from baseball for violating his drug aftercare program. Now Gooden is hoping to salvage his career with the Yankees and help Jeter avoid some of the mistakes he made. "The first thing I told him is that this is the place to be," says Gooden. "There's

nothing wrong with New York. Just be yourself, try to have fun, and this can be a great place to play. I tell Derek that the important thing is to be in front of your locker after every game, good or bad, win or lose. You've got to take the questions head-on. I really think he's ready. He's got the mental toughness. He's a very special breed."

Ordóñez is also a special breed. On July 12, 1993, while competing in the World University Games in Buffalo, Ordóñez made the most memorable move of his baseball career, leaping over a fence and ducking into a red Cadillac. A Cuban radio executive from Miami drove Ordóñez to the airport, and they flew first class to Miami, drinking champagne along the way. Three months later the Mets won his rights in a special lottery for Cuban defectors.

Ordóñez left his father, two sisters, and five brothers in Cuba. He also left his wife, Lisa Maria, and son, Rey Jr., who is now 3½ years old. Since coming to the U.S., Ordóñez has remarried, and he and his wife, Gloryanne, have a nine-month-old daughter named Sonia.

Ordóñez occasionally talks to his father and brothers on the telephone. He says his father, also named Rey, was a better shortstop than he is (he makes about $6 per month working in construction). When asked why he is reluctant to talk about life in Cuba, Ordóñez once said, "The Cuban government reads everything." What does he enjoy the most about life in America? "I just like to go anywhere I want and do what I want," he says.

Has he been disappointed by anything in the first few weeks of his big league career? "I just want to know where all the fans are," he says, noting the low turnout for the Mets' first two homestands. "I thought there would be more people in the stands."

In New York, shortstops come and go faster than classic-rock stations and Thai restaurants. After watching Ordóñez and Jeter on Opening Day, the fans and the media were quick to recall the days when the Yankees had Phil Rizzuto and the Brooklyn Dodgers had

Pee Wee Reese, and New Yorkers lined up behind one shortstop or the other, as if they were following them into battle. That was in the 1940s and '50s. Sometimes it seems New York has been holding shortstop tryouts ever since.

Rizzuto was succeeded by Kubek, a three-time All-Star and the Yankees' last standout at the position. Bucky Dent made the All-Star team as a Yankee in 1980 and '81, but he hit .247 for his career. Jeter was a 1992 first-round draft choice who got a $700,000 signing bonus, and if he hits .247 in New York, not even the panhandlers will go near him. Ordóñez is expected to perform miracles in the field, but Jeter's job might be even tougher. He has to excel on both offense and defense.

Jeter hit .317 at Triple A Columbus last season, but he made 29 errors. It was a vast improvement over the 56 errors he made at Class A Greensboro in 1993 but still is a concern in the Yankees' organization. What if he starts booting balls all over the Stadium? How long will it take before Torre is ordered by George Steinbrenner to sit the kid down or even send him back to Columbus? While Jeter was struggling during spring training, Steinbrenner said, "We'll be patient with him. Every year you look for Derek Jeter to stumble, and he just doesn't. He dominated rookie ball, so we moved him to [Class] A, and he dominated there. We sent him to Double A, and he dominated there. At Columbus it was the same thing. I'm telling you, he could be one of the special ones."

The Mets also believe their long search for a shortstop is over. Harrelson was a defensive stalwart in his 13 seasons with the Mets. Kevin Elster was superb defensively for a couple of seasons in the late '80s before an arm injury led to his departure from the club in 1992. Last season, shortstop José Vizcaíno was voted the team's MVP, but no one was surprised when he was moved to second base to make room for Ordóñez this spring. The next Ozzie Smith doesn't wait on the bench. "He's got great feet,

a great arm," manager Dallas Green says of Ordóñez. "His instincts are tremendous."

Ordóñez hit just .214 in Triple A last season, but he bounced back in the Puerto Rican winter league, hitting .351 and losing the batting title to Roberto Alomar by three points. "I have confidence in my hitting," says Ordóñez. "I only had one bad year, and that was last year. I will get better."

Of course, talking to Ordóñez about hitting is like talking to Cecil Fielder about stealing bases. What's the point? Ordóñez could hold the bat from the wrong end and make sandcastles in the batter's box four times a game, and he would still earn his paycheck with his glove.

"You ask six people to name the best play they ever saw him make, and you'll get six different answers," says Phillips. "A lot of people think that throw from his knees was the best, but one time in the minors he swatted a grounder to first with his glove. Never touched his throwing hand. Another time he grabbed a ground ball behind second and did a pop-up slide on the bag to force the runner. It was the only way he could get his foot on the bag."

With his surprisingly strong arm and graceful footwork, Ordóñez seems to have taken the act of turning a double play to a new level. He glides across the bag as if he were on ice skates and flicks the ball to first as if he were throwing seeds onto the soil. "He does everything so loosely and so spontaneously," says Mets catcher Brent Mayne. "He just feels the flow of the game. Other people stop and think, but the game is too fast to think. You have to just feel it and react, and that's what Rey does."

Mayne has played with Ordóñez for a few weeks now, and he believes Ordóñez could be as good as advertised. "In New York they were calling him the best shortstop ever before he even played a game," says Mayne. "But maybe that's not just a New York thing. Maybe they're right."

Maybe New York finally has a shortstop. Maybe even two. ●

Jeter worked tirelessly to improve his defense early in his career.

By Opening Day 1996, the Yankees were ready to make Jeter their starting shortstop.

He was the team's starting shorstop until he retired in 2014.

The Yankees advanced to the
World Series in Jeter's rookie season,
beating the Orioles in the ALCS.

It was the first of many champagne celebrations for Jeter.

Jeter's RBI single in Game 6
of the 1996 World Series
helped the Yankees claim
their 23rd championship.

Excerpted from SPORTS ILLUSTRATED, February 24, 1997

Long on Shortstops

The Yankees' Derek Jeter is part of a rich crop of young players who are redefining the position

BY TOM VERDUCCI

Measuring Derek Jeter, the 1996 American League Rookie of the Year, against Alex Rodriguez, the league's batting champion, is as unavoidable for the foreseeable future as it is on this February night inside the steamy cinder block gymnasium at the Boys & Girls Club of Miami. "Let's see what you've got," Rodriguez says to Jeter, his friend and foil.

Dressed in jeans and leaning on the bleachers, Jeter is reluctant to take the court. He came here only to watch Rodriguez in one of his regular pickup basketball games, which ended abruptly in its second hour after a hard foul ignited three fistfights, none of which involved the Seattle Mariners shortstop.

Jeter cannot resist the challenge. "All right, Al," he says. The shortstop of the world champion New York Yankees grabs a ball and starts draining jump shots. Within a minute or two, Rodriguez and Jeter are battling each other in a slam-dunk version of H-O-R-S-E. The 6'3", 185-pound Jeter stands flat-footed about four feet from the basket, takes two short steps and easily power slams the basketball—blue jeans be damned. Rodriguez, 6'3" and 205 pounds, matches that move, but he gets

less height on his jump than Jeter does. Rodriguez then stands at the foul line, throws the ball down so that it bounces off the floor and then the backboard, before he catches it and jams it in one vicious swoop. On his first two attempts Jeter fails to get the proper bounce. His third try is only slightly better, and he is left too far from the rim to throw the ball down. "I've got to go," Jeter says, mindful of his flight home to Tampa.

"C'mon with me to New York, DJ," Rodriguez says. He has been trying all evening to persuade Jeter to fly with him the next morning to an awards show, having failed at dinner with his A material: "Cindy's going to be there. Cindy Crawford!"

Jeter insists on leaving, but before he does, he walks to the corner of the court, placing his

heels where the sideline meets the baseline. He heaves a 25-foot jumper. It goes in.

There are many nights on which Rodriguez and Jeter—playing in sold-out ultramodern ballparks around the country—demonstrate why they are state-of-the-art shortstops, possessing an unprecedented combination of size, speed, power, and agility at what historically has been a little man's position. In front of about six people at the Boys & Girls Club of Miami, this, too, is one of those nights.

With Cal Ripken Jr. pushed to third base and Ozzie Smith and Alan Trammell to retirement, there remains only one active shortstop who has started an All-Star Game: Barry Larkin of the Cincinnati Reds, and he turns 33 in April. Fear not for the most crucial position in baseball, though. The best crop of young shortstops to come along in 56 years—and the most multi-talented group ever—already is redefining the position and putting a fresh face on the game.

This week, as most players report to spring training, at least nine teams plan to start a shortstop who is either no older than 23 or has no more than one full season of major league experience. Nomar Garciaparra and Tony Batista, a pair of 23-year-olds who battered Triple A pitching last season before being promoted to the majors, are expected to replace veterans as start-ers for the Boston Red Sox and the Oakland A's, respectively. Benji Gil, 24, a sparkling fielder who missed virtually all of last year because of a back injury, returns as the Texas Rangers' shortstop. Mark Grudzielanek, a late bloomer who turns 27 in June, has a hold on the Montreal Expos' job after his breakout .306 season last year.

At the head of the class are five others who are already setting standards at the position: Rey Ordóñez, 24, of the New York Mets, an acrobat in spikes; Édgar Rentería, 21, of the Florida Marlins, a .309 hitter last season with more range than Cecilia Bartoli; Álex González, 23, of the Toronto Blue Jays, who hit 14 home runs and successfully handled more fielding

chances per nine innings than any other regular shortstop in '96; and Rodriguez, 21, and Jeter, 22, the only shortstops who started 140 games and hit .300 or better with at least 10 home runs last season. Those two are the prototypes of the new generation of shortstops. "I'd love to make an All-Star team," González says, "but with these two guys around, it's going to be real hard over the next 10 or 15 years."

Not since 1941 have so many young short-stops arrived with this much potential. Of the 16 regular shortstops that year, 10 were entering their first or second full season, including three future Hall of Famers: Lou Boudreau, Pee Wee Reese, and Phil Rizzuto. They epito-mized the classic shortstop—short, slick fielders with limited pop at the plate. The average size of the 18 shortstops in the Hall of Fame is 5'10" and 167 pounds.

From 1942 through '73 only two shortstops debuted who would have Hall of Fame careers: Luis Aparicio and Ernie Banks. No shortstop who broke in between Banks (1956) and Robin Yount ('74) is likely to make the Hall of Fame. It was a pitcher-dominated era in which defensive-oriented shortstops such as the Baltimore Orioles' Mark Belanger, a lifetime .228 hitter, carved out long careers.

"In 1966 I was one of five or six shortstops in the [Triple A] International League who were considered future stars," says Yankees scout Gene Michael, a former shortstop. "Mark Belanger, Bud Harrelson, Bobby Murcer, and Gil Garrido were there, too. They called it the year of the shortstop. The only one with pop was Murcer, and he wound up in the outfield. It didn't used to matter if you could hit much."

Yount began a renaissance at the position that was carried on by Trammell (1977), Smith ('78), and the 6'4" Ripken, who in 1982 became the tallest everyday shortstop in history when he was installed there by offensive-minded Baltimore manager Earl Weaver. "Cal Ripken broke the mold," Toronto general manager Gord Ash says.

Rodriguez, who grew up in Miami with a life-sized poster of Ripken in his bedroom, represents the next level of evolution. He is Ripken with speed, not to mention more power and the ability to hit for a higher average. Try to picture Pee Wee and the Scooter staging a slam-dunk competition, and you can understand how far the position has come since 1941. Moreover, most of the top young shortstops today might not even have received the opportunity to play major league ball in '41, six years before Jackie Robinson broke the color barrier. Rodriguez's parents are Dominican. Jeter's father is Black, his mother is white. Ordóñez was born in Cuba, which is also the homeland of González's father. Rentería is one of only four players born in Colombia to have reached the majors.

In 1993, 10 shortstops were playing in their first or second full season in the majors: Mike Bordick, Andújar Cedeño, Royce Clayton, Wil Cordero, Gary DiSarcina, Ricky Gutiérrez, Pat Listach, Pat Meares, José Offerman, and John Valentin. Four years later only three remain at the position with the same club: Valentin (Boston, where he is being pressed by Garciaparra), DiSarcina (Anaheim Angels), and Meares (Minnesota Twins). "There's a big difference this time," Michael says. "That group didn't have the same kind of talent this one does."

"It's cyclical," says Baltimore general manager Pat Gillick about the influx of young shortstops. "Sometimes good players at a position just come in bunches. Shortstop still places a premium on defense. We got Bordick [a free-agent pickup in December] for his defense. But more and more of these young players are turning it into an offensive position."

Rodriguez is bigger than third baseman Mike Schmidt (6'2", 195 pounds) or centerfielder Willie Mays (5'11", 187) were in their prime. Rodriguez's first full season was the best ever by a shortstop. No one who has played the position had more hits (215), more extra-base hits (91), more doubles (54), more total

bases (379), more runs (141), or a better slugging percentage (.631) than he did in 1996. Rodriguez blasted 36 home runs, two fewer than Rizzuto hit in his career, and stole 15 bases, only seven fewer than the Scooter's single-season high. Rodriguez even committed five fewer errors (15) than Cleveland Indians shortstop Omar Vizquel but was runner-up to Vizquel in the Gold Glove Award voting. Imagine if Rodriguez had been healthy all year—he missed 15 days early in the season with a hamstring injury that never fully healed. "I played almost the whole year at about 85 percent," he says. "I expect to steal more bases this year."

Like Rodriguez, Jeter has transfixing green eyes, a tight fade haircut, and physical attributes that send baseball scouts and teenage girls swooning. When Jeter allowed a 14-year-old girl to pose on his lap for a picture at a Yankees fan festival in January, the overwhelmed teen broke into a crying fit.

"We get mistaken for each other all the time," Rodriguez says. The two shortstops talk at least twice a week during the season and share each other's apartments whenever their teams meet. One difference: Jeter is a morning person, Rodriguez is not. One Saturday night last August when Seattle played in New York, Rodriguez told Jeter to wake him the next morning so he could be at Yankee Stadium for a 9:30 workout. Jeter, whose team had no early hitting practice that day, dutifully walked into Rodriguez's room, smacked him on the hip, and said, "C'mon, boy. It's time to get your butt to the ballpark."

"Now that's a friend," Rodriguez says. "That's how much I trust him."

Says Jeter, "I'm Alex's biggest fan. I brag on him so much that my teammates are sick of me talking about him. Last year we talked all the time, especially early in the season. We both knew if we didn't get off to a good start, we might be shipped out."

Actually, Jeter almost didn't make it to Opening Day. With one week left in spring training Yankees owner George Steinbrenner, acting on the advice of his "baseball people," wondered aloud if Jeter was ready and whether the club should trade for an established short-stop. Manager Joe Torre thought it was too late to make such a move. The Yankees stayed with Jeter, who rewarded them by hitting .314, including .350 after the All-Star break. Jeter is not polished defensively—he needs to improve his range moving to his left—but his 22 errors last year represented a huge improvement over the 56 he made in Class A in 1993 and was much better than the 47 charged to Reese in '41. "He weighed 158 pounds when we signed him," Michael says of Jeter, "and he's continued to get bigger and better every year."

Gonzalez is another friend of Rodriguez's—they played high school ball in Miami and in the off-season go out together in search of sail-fish—who brings sock to shortstop. The 6-foot Gonzalez hit the weight room after last season and added nine pounds, bulking up to 195. "My goal this year is to double my numbers in home runs and stolen bases [16]," he says.

The 6'1" Rentería added 10 pounds over the winter and is now 185, though he sheepishly admits to "the McDonald's diet." According to Marlins Latin American scouting director Al Avila, "Rentería is the type of guy who's going to hit .300 year-in and year-out while getting to the point where he should hit 10 to 15 home runs a year." On defense Rentería is so smooth that he makes difficult plays look routine. Only González, Bordick, and Milwaukee's José Valentín gobbled more balls per nine innings last year. "Back home I am like Michael Jordan is here," says Rentería, who was runner-up to the Los Angeles Dodgers' Todd Hollandsworth for National League Rookie of the Year. "The only games on television in Colombia are Marlins games."

The smallish Ordóñez (5'9", 159 pounds), who defected from Cuba in 1993, may not be a hero in his homeland, but he's a favorite of highlight-tape editors across America's television newsrooms. His best glovework is equal to that of Ozzie Smith's. Trouble is, Ordóñez also made 27 errors last year and had a lowly .289 on-base percentage. "Rey has an awful lot to learn about offensive play," says Mets manager Bobby Valentine. "He definitely made too many errors, but most of them came from not being aware of the situation, like the speed of the runner. If it were tennis, he'd have a lot of unforced errors."

Rodriguez, meanwhile, plays the position as if he studied his whole life for it. He is part of America's cable-ready generation, a satellite-fired society bombarded with games. Since he was 11 years old, Rodriguez has watched hundreds of baseball games with a critical eye, absorbing tendencies and habits of players. "When I got to the big leagues," he says, "no one had to tell me that Cal Ripken was a pull hitter or what Darryl Strawberry did with two strikes. My knowledge shortened the learning curve for me, big time."

The next great baseball hero is so young that he cannot remember Ripken playing in the 1983 World Series. "The first one I clearly remember is '84: Tigers-Padres," Rodriguez says. He is so young that only recently did he move out of his mom's house. "I had to," he says. "I didn't fit in my bedroom anymore. I had clothes hanging out of closets and stuff hanging out of windows."

It is past midnight, and Rodriguez, still clad in his basketball clothes, is sitting in the backyard of his new Miami home, an abundance of stars above him. It is a rare moment of repose. In his last week before spring training, Rodriguez will attend three awards dinners (none, alas, at which he will meet Cindy); chat up the folks at *GQ* about a photo spread and a Manhattan advertising firm about a milk ad campaign; do two photo shoots for national magazines, and visit Ripken at his house in Maryland.

Rodriguez's home is not yet fully furnished but displayed prominently in the foyer is a basketball autographed by another of his heroes,

Magic Johnson, who redefined point guard the way Rodriguez is revolutionizing short-stop. Rodriguez grew up watching Magic and the other great basketball stars—Jordan, Bird, and Barkley—enthusiastically sell their sport. Baseball stars are infamous for shirking such ambassadorship, but Rodriguez is equipped to make a difference. Is it fair to ask someone four years removed from high school to be a flag bearer? Did Pee Wee and Scooter have to worry about endorsement strategies, charitable founda-tions, and media training while learning pitchers' tendencies and improving their footwork around the bag?

"I believe the game is just taking off," Rodriguez says, "and maybe as a group we young shortstops can help. The opportunity is there for us. Baseball always comes first, though. You're in trouble the minute you start thinking you're a media strategist or marketing guy and not a baseball player.

"I want to get better. I love it when people say that last season was a career year for me, that I can't do it again. I love to hear people say that. That's a challenge to me, a major challenge."

Rodriguez, still revving as if it were noon, walks into his den and pops a highlight tape into his VCR. A coffee-table book about Joe Montana is so worn that its cover curls perpetually open. Rodriguez is a voracious reader whose tastes run to the motivational tomes of Pat Riley and Anthony Robbins. The tape begins with a title, *Alex Rodriguez. Hitting. 1996.* Sitting on a kitchen chair turned backward, he faces the big-screen TV with his chin resting on his crossed arms atop the chair back. His eyes, like his house, are aglow. He is alone with his perfect, edited self. Every pitch is a swing. Every swing is a hit. ●

Jeter appeared largely unbothered by playing under the bright lights of New York.

Friends, opponents at the 1997 MTV's Rock and Jock Softball Challenge in 1997, and future teammates Alex Rodriguez and Derek Jeter.

Jeter sits in the dugout between coach Don Zimmer and manager Joe Torre.

Jeter welcomes Tino Martinez at home plate after the first baseman's home run against San Diego in Game 1 of the 1998 World Series.

Jeter homered in Game 4 and the Yankees swept the Padres for the franchise's 24th championship.

Excerpted from SPORTS ILLUSTRATED, June 21, 1999

Prince of the City

Gotham loves its real Bat Man, Yankees shortstop Derek Jeter, who's got what it takes—looks, poise, talent—to be the top banana in the Big Apple

BY MICHAEL SILVER

He's the master of his metropolis, but sometimes the Big Apple bites back. One evening last month New York Yankees shortstop Derek Jeter went shopping for a videocassette recorder and encountered some serious static. When a salty salesman—we'll call him Manuel—at Circuit City on East 86th Street told Jeter, "You suck," it seemed like an appropriate time for extra batting practice.

The beef began after Manuel struck out trying to locate a VCR that Jeter wanted to purchase, the store computer indicating that each of the player's first three selections were out of stock. After Jeter settled for his fourth choice, he was told by Manuel to follow him to another register because Manuel's had malfunctioned.

"Doesn't anything work in this store?" Jeter joked. "My credit card doesn't work either."

Perhaps Manuel has an offbeat sense of humor, or perhaps he was having a bad day, but this was his response: "Yeah, well, you suck anyway."

Jeter did a double take. "I suck?" he said.

"Yeah, you suck," Manuel said. "Griffey's better."

"Yeah?" Jeter said. "Do I come to your job and tell you some other guy is better than you?"

"What, did I offend you?" the salesman replied.

"No, not at all," Jeter said, his voice rising, his green eyes ablaze with anger. "I like hearing that I suck."

A few seconds later Jeter regained his composure. "Welcome to New York," he said to an out-of-town shopping companion. "Now I've officially heard it all. I come to this store to spend money, and the salesman tells me I suck. Nothing in this town surprises me anymore."

Manuel handed Jeter the sales receipt, grinning a goofy grin. Charles Barkley might have tossed the guy through the 31-inch TV set

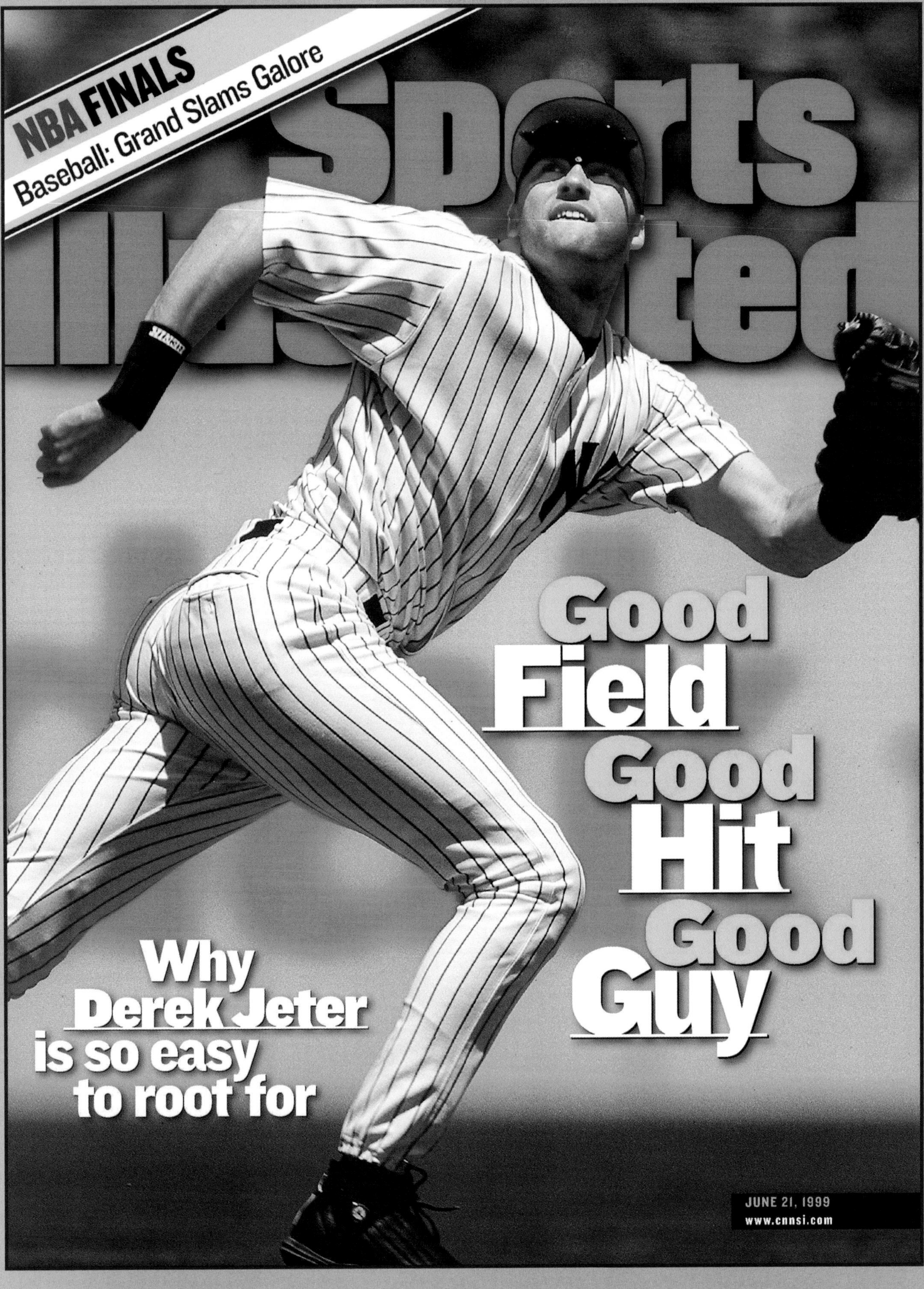

NBA FINALS
Baseball: Grand Slams Galore
Sports Illustrated
Good Field Good Hit Good Guy
Why Derek Jeter is so easy to root for
JUNE 21, 1999
www.cnnsi.com

behind the register. Jeter just smiled and said, "Have a nice day."

That's life in the big city, but for Jeter it's a mere speck of lint on his red carpet. The handsome, personable, and relentlessly polite baseball star, who turns 25 on June 26, is bigger than Austin Powers. Driving to Yankee Stadium he's occasionally pulled over by cops asking for his autograph. When he comes to bat, teenage girls shriek as if he were a Beatle landing in the U.S. 35 years ago. Gossip columnists, still frothing over Jeter's past romance with pop diva Mariah Carey, document his every social step—and some he's never taken.

In only his fourth full major league season, Jeter is New York's most adored ballplayer in at least a decade, possibly since Reggie Jackson led the Yankees to back-to-back world championships in the late '70s. Anointed by Michael Jordan as his Air Apparent at Nike— he signed a lucrative deal with Jordan's new brand within a brand—Jeter, by virtue of his performance, personality, looks, and location, is positioned for megastardom.

"If you're looking for complaints, I don't have any," he says. "Okay, the traffic here is a pain, but other than that, I'm living a dream. I think I'm the luckiest person in the world."

If he sounds suspiciously like Lou Gehrig, it's appropriate. While most of New York's sports superstars have modeled themselves on fun-loving, cocksure Babe Ruth—from Mickey Mantle and Joe Namath to Jackson and Lawrence Taylor—Jeter springs from the Gehrig branch of the family tree, emulating the Yankee slugger's graceful, understated dignity. Shy and protective of his image, Jeter is accessible to fans and the press but keeps a small circle of close friends. He has been embraced by celebrity more than he has embraced it.

Gotham's love for this bat man is reciprocated. "This is the greatest city in the world," Jeter says as he peers out toward the East River from the living room of his Upper East Side apartment. "You always hear players say, 'I'd never play in New York.' I don't understand why you'd say that—unless you're afraid to fail."

Not much chance of that happening to Jeter. In 1996 he became the first rookie in 34 years to start at shortstop for the Yankees, won Rookie of the Year honors, and hit .361 in the post-season. Last season he finished third in the American League MVP balloting, and the Yankees won their second World Series in three years. This season he's one of the league's most productive players. At week's end he ranked second in batting (.380), tied for first in hits (89), tied for fourth in runs (54), first in triples (seven), and second in on-base percentage (.471), and his power numbers—11 homers, 43 RBIs, .658 slugging percentage—were well up from last year, when he finished with 19 homers and 84 RBIs in 149 games. He reached base at least once in each of the Yankees' first 53 games and, with his exceptional range in the field, made enough sensational plays to more than compensate for his eight errors. (He had nine last season, a career low.)

Jeter's early MVP candidacy has been endorsed by another heavy hitter: the Seattle Mariners' Alex Rodriguez, who with 42 homers last season set an American League record for shortstops. Rodriguez, 23, who missed all but two games in the first five weeks of this season with a knee injury, seems to have been indirectly responsible for his good friend Jeter's power surge. "A friendly rivalry can motivate you," Rodriguez says.

Says Milwaukee Brewers manager Phil Garner, "I thought A-Rod was way ahead of Jeter, that he was always going to be a better [all-around] player. But now Jeter has come on and caught him."

Jeter, who owns a home near the Yankees' training facility in Tampa, spent much of the off-season lifting weights and fine-tuning his swing. During a three-game series with the Mariners during the weekend of May 7–9, as the rehabbing Rodriguez watched from the visitors' dugout at Yankee Stadium, Jeter showed off his new muscle. He smacked a three-run homer on Friday night and then, in the first inning of the Yankees' victory on Sunday, drove a 1-1 fastball from lefthander Jeff Fassero 430 feet over the fence in left centerfield. That game featured a typical display of Jeter's all-around excellence: he singled to lead off the fifth inning and promptly stole second, and in the seventh he deftly stabbed a sharp grounder to start an inning-ending double play. But it was the homer that stood out.

"That's a pitch that in the past I wouldn't have hit for a home run," the budding slugger said the next day as he scarfed down chicken parmigiana at an Italian restaurant. "I've learned to turn on the ball a little more. I used to inside-out a lot of balls to rightfield, but now I drive them using more of my top hand. In the off-season I worked with our minor league coaches and changed some things mechanically. But my body is still maturing, and I have a long way to go in terms of strength. I'm not trying to hit 42 home runs this year, that's for sure."

Impressive as they are, mere numbers don't do Jeter's game justice. Assessing his talent is like describing Lucille Ball's comic timing: everything he does, from his cutoff throw to his home run trot, is unerringly smooth. And Jeter, a first-round draft pick out of Kalamazoo (Mich.) Central High in 1992, keeps refining his game.

"He's the best player I've ever played with, and I think a lot of people in this clubhouse are going to say that before he's done," says Paul O'Neill, the Yankees' 36-year-old right-fielder. "What sets him apart is the number of ways he can affect a game."

Jeter's increased patience at the plate and his improved power have created a quandary for pitchers. "You can throw him inside as much as you want, and he can still fist the ball off," says Baltimore Orioles veteran reliever Jesse Orosco. "You can throw the ball low and away, and he

can hit with power the other way. We have pitchers' meetings, and he's one of those guys where you just stay on the subject for a while. What do you do?"

Jeter's personality is as polished as his game. The Yankees have been captainless since Don Mattingly retired after the '95 season. Jeter, at least unofficially, has emerged as Mattingly's successor. "In some ways he already is the captain," says veteran righthander David Cone. "He's very mature and grounded."

As a rookie Jeter earned instant respect in the clubhouse by playing hard and keeping his mouth shut, but now he is more vocal with his off-key singing and his in-your-face teasing. He has attempted to fill the void left by the departure of veteran outfielder Tim Raines, whose ebullience helped keep the Yankees loose. But Jeter can also speak sternly, as he did last September to lefthander David Wells (now with the Toronto Blue Jays) after Wells gestured angrily when Jeter and two other players allowed a pop-up to fall among them. Recalls Jeter, "I told him, 'We're out here trying to help you win a game. We don't show you up, so don't do it to us.' I'm not afraid to speak my mind. There have been a lot of other instances, but I don't think the media needs to know about them."

Because Jeter has impeccable manners, he's a role model even to his elders. Who else could inspire George Steinbrenner and Darryl Strawberry to say, "He's the kind of guy you hope your son can grow up to be"? Strawberry, who's on administrative leave from baseball after pleading no contest to charges of cocaine possession and soliciting a prostitute in Florida, says that Jeter "has a great deal of respect for everyone he encounters. That's what sets him apart."

All this explains Jeter's immense popularity among his peers, but it can't account for the screams that fill Yankee Stadium when his name is announced or for the female fans who paint I

LOVE DJ on their faces—the Jeterettes, as the *New York Daily News* dubbed them. Even if he were merely a baseball-loving stockbroker, the 6'3", 195-pounder would be a chick magnet. "Hanging out with him sucks," says Chili Davis, his 39-year-old teammate, "because all the women flock to him. Let's see, he's been on the cover of *GQ*, is rich and famous, hits for average and power, and is a helluva nice guy."

If he wanted, Jeter could have a little black book the size of the Yellow Pages. "Every time he steps into a room, all eyes start turning to him—that even goes for women who are with their dates," says Raines, now with the Oakland A's. "Usually the guys don't mind because they're staring at him too."

"I call him a movie star because he runs the town," says Rodriguez, a highly eligible bachelor himself. "But the thing that impresses me most about him is that he's so selective—not just with girls, but with people in general."

Unless you're a teammate, family member, or close friend, expect Jeter to put up a wall when you approach him. That's partly because of his natural reticence and partly because he feels he has been burned by spiced-up tabloid tales of his gallivanting. At the ballpark Jeter prides himself on being unfailingly cordial and cooperative with the media. "I don't agree with people who, when they're playing well, walk around with their chests puffed out and wait for reporters at their locker, but who hide in the training room as soon as things go bad," he says. Get Jeter away from the ballpark and ask about his social life, though, and he's as uneasy as a batter facing Randy Johnson with an 0-and-2 count.

Derek, what's it like when you go clubbing downtown?

Blank stare. "I don't really go out," he says. "I'm a big movie fan. That's basically what I do every night, even in the off-season. Dinner and a movie. I'm a homebody."

Jeter has a two-bedroom apartment in a relatively modest high-rise, and this is what you see in the living room: a couch, a TV, a laptop computer propped up on an empty box. In the kitchen there are two basic nutritional options: Wheaties and Apple Jacks. It sure doesn't look like a crib in which someone spends a lot of time hanging.

Thumb through a stack of clips on Jeter, and his concern for his privacy makes more sense. Drawing mostly from the *New York Post*'s Page Six and the *Daily News*' gossip section, you read that Jeter's romance with Carey began in the fall of '96, while she was still married to record executive Tommy Mottola; that early in the '98 season Steinbrenner warned Jeter to cool things with Carey because the Yankees' owner felt that the relationship was hurting his player's game; that one night during last year's pennant race Jeter showed up at Moomba with a group of athletes and then went on to the China Club and partied into the wee hours. Then, while attending rap artist-producer Sean (Puffy) Combs' birthday party at a Wall Street restaurant last November, the papers say, Jeter continually rebuffed Carey's flirtatious advances. (In April the *New York Observer* revealed that the verb "to jeter" had entered the city's lexicon as a "synonym for 'to diss' or 'to blow off,' as in: He jetered her big time.")

Who knows how much of this is true, but Jeter clearly resents gossip and says that an awful lot of what's been written about him is false. "One time I was in Puerto Rico, and my mom heard on the radio that I was out doing this or that with some person at a ridiculous hour, at some place I'd never been before," he says shrugging.

On the other hand, he's smart enough to understand that he invited the attention by carrying on with Carey, with whom he says he is still friendly. (She declined to be interviewed for this article.) "It's hard for me to have a relationship the way things are right now," he says. "I'd have to be with someone very understanding, someone who's willing to deal with all the attention. But going out with Mariah, that's taking it to a whole other level. She's someone who's known worldwide. I don't see how two very famous people—and I'm nowhere close to her level—would be able to deal with that over the long haul. It's too much."

Jeter says he has been in love once—with his high school girlfriend, from whom he drifted apart. He insists that he doesn't date much, that his schedule lends itself more to going out in groups and that he worries about finding a woman who loves him for who he is rather than what he is. He has a built-in safeguard against getting suckered. Two, actually. "I think I'm a pretty good judge of character," he says, "but even if you fool me, you've got to get by my mom and my sister. It takes a lot to pass that test."

Derek's mother, Dorothy, an accountant, laughs when that statement is relayed to her. "He does a lot of screening before we even get involved," she says. "There are just certain things you can tell about a person—sometimes it might even be her name, or her hair."

Derek's 19-year-old sister, Sharlee, a student at Atlanta's Spelman College, has a long history of looking out for her big brother. "There's this incident I still get teased about," she says. "At one of his high school baseball games I confronted this girl he was dating. I was in the sixth or seventh grade, and I said to her, 'I don't want you here, and Derek doesn't want you here.' I think I was just jealous that she was taking my brother away from me, but even now I'm really protective.

"I ended up loving Mariah Carey to death, but I would've taken her on, too, if she hadn't measured up. People said, 'Oooh, it's Mariah Carey, that's perfect.' I was like, I don't know who she is. I know how she is on TV, but that doesn't tell me anything. So, yeah, she still had to go through the Test, and yeah, she passed. I think she was forewarned."

Dorothy tells her son he should frequent bookstores because, she says, "that's a good place to meet girls—but don't write that, because then they'll all start hanging out in there."

Derek has his own peculiar screening technique. "One thing he likes to do when he meets a girl is ask very difficult questions," says Douglas Biro, a Tampa-based professional golfer who has been close to Jeter since they met in

> "This is the greatest city in the world," Jeter says as he peers out toward the East River from the living room of his Upper East Side apartment. "You always hear players say, 'I'd never play in New York.' I don't understand why you'd say that—unless you're afraid to fail."

the fourth grade in Kalamazoo. "He'll ask a hypothetical question, usually along ethical lines. It can be really funny—I've seen women get flustered because they have to play along—but I think he really does it to find out a person's true colors."

"It can be really funny, because the female doesn't have any idea what he's thinking," says Atlanta Braves outfielder Gerald Williams, Jeter's former Yankees teammate. "It's usually about how she would handle a certain situation. He's trying to find out if she would lose her cool and rant and rave, or stay calm and keep her dignity. He's not looking for someone who exhibits extreme behavior, a woman who would bring unnecessary attention to herself, because there's already enough attention [on him] as it is. He wants a woman he can be comfortable with wherever they are, no matter what's going on around them."

Jeter's up in his apartment on a night off, watching Latrell Sprewell and Tim Hardaway go at it in a Knicks-Heat game on TV, when suddenly his eyes drift to his window. "There's someone doing Tae-Bo," he says, gesturing to an apartment across the street. Sure enough, a young woman can be seen performing the trendy workout. "It's a long way from Kalamazoo," he says laughing.

Ask Jeter about his background, and his mood brightens. "You've got to know my family," he says. "My upbringing was like *The Cosby Show*. We had fun, always did a lot of things together. My parents were involved in everything my sister and I did."

Before every school year Charles and Dorothy Jeter required Derek and Sharlee to sign a handwritten contract that spelled out, among other things, their study habits (daily), expected grades (A's), chores (many), curfew (early), and rules regarding alcohol and drugs (forget about it). "I always tried to negotiate," Sharlee says, "but Derek just sat there and nodded. It was hard having this older brother

who did everything he was supposed to do. He had a lot of friends who could do whatever they wanted—stay out late, even the night before a game—but our curfews were always the earliest."

Derek was both sheltered and shy. "When he was 12 or 13, I took him to a basketball camp at the University of Michigan, and when it was time for him to meet the other kids, I had to push him to make conversation," says Charles, a drug-and-alcohol-abuse counselor with a Ph.D., who gave up his practice a year and a half ago to run his son's charitable foundation. "When he was in the eighth grade and was about to switch from parochial school to a public school, we sent him over to the Y to play basketball against older kids as a way of toughening him up. He went, but he took his mother with him."

Now Jeter endorses Coach leather goods, Florsheim shoes, Fleet Bank, Nike, and Skippy peanut butter—and the list is likely to grow. "He's doing as well as probably any other player in baseball," says his agent, Casey Close, "and we've turned down a lot of things."

Earlier this year Jordan chose Jeter as the lead endorser for Brand Jordan at Nike. "I love his work ethic," says Jordan, who met Jeter in '94 while playing in the Arizona Fall League during his hiatus from basketball. "He has a great attitude. He has the qualities that separate superstars from everyday people, and a lot of it is attributable to his great family background."

Like Jordan, Jeter has obvious crossover appeal, though it's not clear to which side he's crossing over. The son of a Black father from Alabama and an Irish American mother from northern New Jersey, Jeter says that often "people think I'm Hispanic." More important, he tries to pass on his good fortune to others. After his rookie season, Jeter—inspired by his childhood idol, former Yankees outfielder Dave Winfield, who started a foundation for underprivileged children—established the

Turn 2 Foundation, which works to steer high-risk kids away from drugs.

Another of Jeter's endearing traits is his nonjudgmental nature, as evidenced by his choice of mentors—including Raines, who battled a cocaine addiction early in his career, and Strawberry. At spring training in '97, following Jeter's rookie year, Strawberry sat the kid down, warned him that expectations would be higher this time around, and cautioned him not to feel pressured to carry the team. "Darryl Strawberry has been like a big brother to me," Jeter says. "If anyone can relate to what I'm going through, being the big man around here, it's him."

"I told him early on to avoid the pitfalls that plagued me," Strawberry says. "New York is a place that can swallow you up if you're not able to handle the pressure of success—and of failure. He handles it with class and dignity."

So what's a person and player as good as Jeter worth on the open market? An arbitrator awarded him a '99 salary of $5 million, which will seem like tip money if he files for free agency following the 2001 season. "With the way he's playing and improving," says Cincinnati Reds general manager Jim Bowden, "there's no reason he won't be able to get $15 million to $20 million a year."

In all likelihood the Yankees will fork over enough cash before then to secure Jeter's long-term commitment. He won't be a tough sell. He grew up worshiping the team, and he still occasionally gets choked up when he walks from the Yankees' clubhouse to the field and sees a sign above the tunnel inscribed with a quote from Joe DiMaggio: "I WANT TO THANK THE GOOD LORD FOR MAKING ME A YANKEE."

What Jeter loves about New York is more than just the baseball, though. It's the pizza that folds over and the go-for-broke driving and the time he saw Spike Lee shooting a commercial at Yankee Stadium before a game and said to the sports-loving director, "When are you going to let me be in one of your movies?"

"Can you act?" Lee asked. Jeter nodded.

"Well, act like a shortstop tonight."

Jeter chuckles at the recollection as he crawls toward downtown in a stretch limousine that's taking him to a photo shoot. In some ways he is like this vehicle: sleek and attention-grabbing. Everyone wants to get a good look inside, but only a privileged few are allowed that opportunity.

The limo comes to a halt across the street from City Hall. Rudy Giuliani may be the mayor, but Jeter could own this town, if only he'd get out more. You remind him of the homebody comment, and finally he lets down his guard. "Look, I'm like every other 24-year-old," he says. "This city is a melting pot, and the women here are the most beautiful in the world. Every night here is a Friday night—the places you go are going to be packed. During the season it's difficult to get into a pattern of going out, because the places are great, you lose track of time, and all of a sudden it's 5 or 6 a.m. Baseball's a game in which it's real easy to tell if you've been out late the previous night, so I have to pick my spots. But during the off-season, when I'm here, it's a totally different story."

Jeter lowers the window of the limo, and passersby take to him as if to a long-lost cousin. A college student takes a term paper from her book bag and hands it to Jeter. "Can you sign it, please?" she says. "I don't care if it's due today." Minutes later a city bus passes the limo and screeches to a stop in the middle of the street, in rush-hour traffic. Risking life and limb, the bus driver jumps out, rushes to the limo, and hands Jeter a transit slip to sign.

The driver resumes his post without incident, and as the bus pulls away, Jeter pounds his fist on the leather interior. "Whaddaya think of that?" he asks his out-of-town visitor.

The prince of the city is in his element. It definitely doesn't suck. •

Jeter travels through
Manhattan in style in 1999.

At the 1999 All-Star Game, the second of Jeter's 14 career selections.

Jeter feeling at home in
Little Italy in 1999.

Excerpted from SPORTS ILLUSTRATED, November 1, 1999

October's Guy

After just four years in the big leagues, Derek Jeter is building a postseason record for the ages

BY STEPHEN CANNELLA

In the moments before Game 2, during the ceremonies announcing baseball's All-Century team, Derek Jeter stood on the top step of the New York Yankees' dugout, peering out over the railing and applauding as each hero was introduced to the Turner Field crowd. Jeter is wrapping up just his fourth full big league season, but he might have found more than a few of those greats willing to trade careers with him.

For all the honorees' statistical wattage, Jeter, the New York shortstop, has something many of them lacked: a knack for postseason constancy and accomplishment that would make King Midas blush and reduce Ernie Banks to tears. Granted, Jeter's numbers are swelled by extra playoff rounds that didn't exist for most of the century, but they are staggering nonetheless. He took the field for the 12th time in a World Series and the 43rd time in the postseason on Sunday night, meaning that at the tender age of 25, Jeter, a career .329 postseason hitter, had already played more postseason games than 16 of the 21 position players on the All-Century roster. If the Yankees hold the 2–0 lead they built over the

Atlanta Braves last weekend, Jeter would be the first player since divisional play began in 1969 to win three world championships by age 25.

"He's played his whole career in the World Series," says New York designated hitter Chili Davis, who has made three trips to the Fall Classic in his 19-year career. "To him this is just how major league baseball should be, and anything else would be wrong. If he played a year when he didn't go to the playoffs, he'd probably go home and cry and wonder what happened."

"I think it's ironic that my first year, 1995, was [Don] Mattingly's last year," says Jeter, who played 15 games for the Yankees that

Jeter and the Yankees celebrate Jim Leyritz's home run in Game 4 of the 1999 World Series.

year but was not on the roster for New York's Division Series loss to the Seattle Mariners. "That was the only postseason he went to. I realize it's difficult to get here. I've just been very fortunate to be on good teams."

Fortunate, yes, but Jeter hasn't exactly been riding coattails. He attacks playoff pitching the way a child prodigy breezes through the PSATs. His performance in the Yankees' 7–2 Game 2 win on Sunday night—2-for-5, two runs scored—extended his postseason hitting streak to 15 games, the third longest in history. (Hank Bauer of the Yankees holds the record of 17.) With 57 hits in 43 games, Jeter had already roughly equaled the postseason accomplishments of Joe DiMaggio, who had 54 hits in 51 games, albeit all in the World Series. In Series play Jeter had 15 hits in 12 games and was averaging .326 and a run per game. In New York's 10 straight Series wins from Game 3 in 1996 through Game 2 this year, Jeter had gone 14-for-41. After going 4-for-9 last weekend, he was hitting .400 (16-for-40) in the 1999 postseason, with an on-base percentage of .467.

"I don't treat these games any differently from any others," says Jeter, who finished second in the American League batting race this season, at .349. "I just relax because the great thing about baseball is if you strike out or make an error, you come back the next day to redeem yourself."

Or in his case, next October. •

Watching a close pitch against the Braves in the 1999 World Series.

The Yankees swept the Braves in the 1999 World Series for their third championship in four years.

RISE OF THE CAPTAIN

A legend among legends:
Jeter spends a quiet moment
in Monument Park.

Chapter 2

Jeter and José Vizcaíno
embrace after winning
Game 1 of the
2000 World Series
against the Mets.

Excerpted from Sports Illustrated, November 6, 2000

The Toast of the Town

After leading the Yankees to another World Series title, cool yet fiercely competitive Derek Jeter owns Yankee Stadium—and the rest of New York City—the way no player since Joe DiMaggio has

BY TOM VERDUCCI

"Where are my parents? Where are my parents?"

In and out of spikes, New York Yankees shortstop Derek Jeter moves like silk billowed by a breeze. Goodness flows all around him. He's perpetually light on his feet, even as bedlam spills like the champagne in and around the dank hallways of Shea Stadium early last Friday in the afterglow of—goodness!—the Yankees' fourth world championship in Jeter's five full seasons in the big leagues.

At 26, he has already been enriched with a lifetime's heaping portion of success.

"Mr. Jeter, this is the police commissioner. Would you like a picture [with him]?" asks a police officer outside the Yankees clubhouse, introducing Jeter to Bernard Kerik, the new commissioner of the New York City Police Department. The hallway is a gridlock of people. Jeter, the champagne still dripping from his uniform, flashes his golden grin, as if he is lit from within like a paper lantern.

"I've got a couple of parking tickets I'd like to talk to you about," Jeter says as he glides past the commish.

Smooth. Kerik laughs. "We'll talk," he says.

Jeter doesn't linger. "Where are my parents? Find out where they are," he says to a Yankees security official, who squawks into his radio to another official.

Every time Derek plays a baseball game attended by his parents, Charles and Dorothy of Kalamazoo, Mich., he must know where they are seated. Before the first ball is put into play, he catches their gaze and gives them a wave of his hand. He must know where they are after the game, too. On this night, before the Yankees' 4–2 Game 5 victory that clinched the World Series, Jeter found them in their distant seats high above

Jeter scores the tying run past Mets catcher Mike Piazza in Game 3 of the 2000 World Series.

third base. Afterward, in the madness, he cannot locate them. Then the radio answers, "Right by me. On the field."

Jeter skips along the creaky wooden runway that leads through the darkness under Shea's field-level seats to the dugout. To no one in particular he says aloud with a sigh, "Oh, man. If we'd lost this, I was moving out of town. Gone!" He bolts up the dugout steps, where he finds his parents standing on the warning track. He gives them each a kiss and a long, tight hug.

"MVP! MVP!" A large knot of fans behind the Yankees dugout begins serenading him with the latest of his many honorifics. Jeter had at least one crucial hit or play in each of the Yankees' four wins in their defeat of their crosstown rivals, the Mets, earning himself the World Series MVP award. It will make a nice bookend to his All-Star Game MVP award. No other player has ever won both awards in the same season.

Jeter tosses several championship caps into the crowd. Then he dashes back toward the clubhouse, heaving his jersey for safekeeping at a friend in the corridor. He will give it to his mother as a gift.

After showering, Jeter puts on a silvery gray, windowpane suit with a gray silk T-shirt underneath. The man is impervious to wrinkles. He walks out of the clubhouse and down a long, curved hallway that empties into the visitors' bullpen in leftfield, where New York City mayor Rudy Giuliani is playing catch on the back mound and tenor Placido Domingo is dodging manure deposited by horses of the mounted police. Domingo excitedly greets Jeter. "I called it! Your home run!" says Domingo, who keeps stride with Jeter as the shortstop walks along the warning track toward an open gate in the centerfield fence. "I turned to the mayor's son, Andy, just before you hit it. I said, 'Derek's going to hit a home run!' I did! I called it!"

"Wish I knew," Jeter says, smiling.

"Watch the manure!" yells a security official. "You might want to stay off the track. There's a ton of it."

"Nah. No problem," Jeter says.

As he walks out the gate, Jeter is saluted with a polite ovation from several laborers who are taking apart scaffolding. One of them yells, "Derek, you're spoiling us!"

There, behind the giant black centerfield background for hitters, Jeter slips into a white stretch limo that whisks him to a private party at One51, a Manhattan club. The club has velvet ropes and bouncers behind them. The place is an

> **It's in DiMaggio's footsteps that Jeter walks proudly and gracefully. The rare modern player who has never tried creatine or yearned for muscle mass, the 6'3", 195-pound Jeter has the smooth carriage and angular build of a baseball player from DiMaggio's era.**

elbow-to-elbow hothouse of smoke, body heat, and music so loud you can feel your heart quake. Hardly anyone dances, though. Jeter is ensconced in the inner sanctum, a raised area next to the dance floor. Almost everyone is turned toward him in a kind of homage that spookily resembles idolatry. Women try to push and lie their way past the no-necked, square-headed keepers of the last velvet rope.

Teammates David Justice, Denny Neagle, and Luis Polonia are there, too, but nobody pays them much notice. When Jeter walks across the dance floor to the raised area on the other side, the simple act takes on the complexity of a military maneuver. The men without necks part the room, either commanding people to move out of the way or just shoving women. But, hey, what's a little humiliation in the name of idolatry? One woman, drinking her money's worth, boasts that she paid $12,000 to reserve one of the few tables in the inner sanctum.

Jeter is a wallflower, a bit uncomfortable with the size of the crowd but enjoying the beat of the music and the company of close friends. Mostly, while standing on a long sofa against the wall, he chats with his sister, Sharlee, and his steady, Lara Dutta, who hails from Bangalore, India, and who happens to be Miss Universe. Others, including Justice, also lean against the wall, the better to survey the room. Friends come and go with their congratulations. Jeter offers them flutes of champagne, though he takes none for himself. It will be 5 a.m. by the time he leaves, with television cameras still waiting out front to get a glimpse of him and the other Yankees.

This is the night Jeter's status as a baseball icon has become official. Never mind One51. An athlete can play no bigger room than the domain of Yankees baseball. Right now Jeter owns the room.

Once upon a time there was a man named DiMaggio who played baseball with such graceful ease that people swore they'd never see his like again. DiMaggio was, above all, a winner.

His Yankees—and, yes, the New York teams from 1936 to '41, the Clipper's first six seasons in the major leagues, were known as DiMaggio's Yankees—won 598 games, approaching 100 a year, and failed to win the World Series only once.

It's in DiMaggio's footsteps that Jeter walks proudly and gracefully. The rare modern player who has never tried creatine or yearned for muscle mass, the 6'3", 195-pound Jeter has the smooth carriage and angular build of a baseball player from DiMaggio's era. Jeter, above all, is a winner too. His Yankees—and, yes, this dynasty will go down as Jeter's Yankees—have won 487 games, approaching 100 a year, and have failed to win the World Series only once. Over five postseasons they have played .754 baseball, going 46–15. Only one other team in history besides DiMaggio's Yankees (who won consecutive World Series from 1936 to '39) and Jeter's Yankees has won as many titles in a five-year span, and that club, the 1949 to '53 Yankees, did it while the torch passed from DiMaggio to Mickey Mantle in '51, midway through its unmatched run of five straight championships.

"I met him a couple of times when he came out to the Stadium," Jeter says of DiMaggio, "but I never had a conversation with him. I shook his hand, said hello, but I was too much in awe to talk to him."

Now Jeter is DiMaggio's worthy heir, in style and in numbers. In regular-season and World Series play, DiMaggio scored 625 runs through his fifth full season. Jeter scored 623. DiMaggio had 994 hits. Jeter had 1,034. DiMaggio played in 19 World Series games over his first five seasons; his Yankees went 16–3. Jeter played in 19 World Series games, too; his Yankees went 16–3. Jeter hit for a higher World Series batting average (.342) than did DiMaggio (.304), while producing more of New York's offense than Joltin' Joe: from 1936 to '39, DiMaggio scored or drove in 21 of the Yankees' 113 runs in the World Series, or 19%;

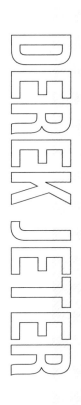

from 1996 through 2000, Jeter was responsible for 22 of New York's 85 Series runs, or 26%.

Through five seasons the ring count is all even. Jeter keeps his rings locked away at his home in Tampa. Once after each season he will take them out to study them. "Each one tells a different story, like chapters in a book," he says. "Starting in November, when you begin to work out, through October you devote a whole year to do one thing: to win. That's all that matters. This is the way I've always looked at it: if you're going to play at all, you're out to win. Baseball, board games, playing along with *Jeopardy!* with my friends. I hate to lose."

Jeter seemed destined for greatness. He shares a birthday (June 26) with Abner Doubleday, the mythical inventor of baseball. On the day the Yankees' front office gathered to talk about its top pick of the 1992 draft, Jeter's name came up, and one of those present said, "Jeter? Isn't he going to Michigan?" There was a moment of silence. Then Dick Groch, the scout who signed Jeter, said, "No. He's going to Cooperstown."

Says Reggie Jackson, the original Mr. October, "In big games, the action slows down for him where it speeds up for others. I've told him, 'I'll trade my past for your future.'"

Jeter always has played with a cool assuredness beyond his years. In 1996, at 22 and in his first World Series, he told manager Joe Torre during a meeting on the mound in Game 4, when the Yankees trailed the Atlanta Braves 6–0, "Don't worry. We're going to win this game." The Yankees did, 8–6, the second of 14 straight World Series wins, a record that Mets manager Bobby Valentine last week said will stand longer than DiMaggio's 56-game hitting streak.

"This kid, right now, the tougher the situation, the more fire he gets in his eyes," Torre said before Game 5. "You don't teach that. It's something you have to be born with. His parents are a big part of that."

Says Jeter, "I try not to change anything in the postseason. I don't like to say you focus more in the postseason, because that sounds like you're focusing less during the season. But in the postseason you are more focused. You can't help it. Every pitch, every grounder, every inning means more.

"Now, what I try to do is keep it simple, treat it like a regular-season game. Obviously you're going to have more butterflies. But I don't feel like I act any differently because it's the postseason. What I'm proud of is that I try to stay on an even keel. That is something I learned from my parents."

He has been making these Yankees his team for years, but it was on Sept. 29, two days before the end of the regular season, that he stepped forward like never before. Torre held a pregame meeting that night, with the Yankees reeling from 12 losses in 15 games. He ended his short talk by saying, "Does anybody have anything to say?"

Silence hung in the air. Then Jeter stood and addressed the team as a whole for the first time. "Everyone is trying to do too much," he said. "We've always won because guys just did their jobs, and if they didn't, they knew the next guy would get it done. We've always used 25 guys to win. We have to get back to that. People have got to stop trying to do it by themselves." No one else added a word.

This World Series elevated his stature, especially because of what was at stake. In the days leading up to the Subway Series, Mets fans jammed on their car brakes if they saw him exit his Manhattan apartment and shouted, "Jeter, you suck!" Yankees fans would tell him, "Whatever you do, don't lose to the Mets."

"We had a lot to lose," Jeter says. "I'm serious: I would have moved right out of the city if we'd lost. You could have taken our three rings and thrown them out the window, as far as Yankees fans were concerned. I'm glad I played in a Subway Series, but maybe once is enough."

Jeter admitted to bouts of nervousness in this Series, during the times he played shortstop on

Shea Stadium's notoriously awful infield. The field is so bumpy that Jeter would tell coaches to quit hitting him practice grounders before games. "You'd start getting scared and lose your confidence," he says. "I'll tell you, they need to cut Bill Buckner some slack. I was out there thinking, You can strike out, get picked off, do anything, but don't let a ground ball go through your legs. I was going to get down and block it if I had to." Characteristically, Jeter didn't make an error in the Series and hasn't committed one in the Fall Classic since '96.

Jeter helped mightily in every Yankees win. In the pivotal play of Game 1, a 4–3 nail-biter that the Yankees won in 12 innings, he threw out the Mets' fleet Timo Pérez at the plate in the sixth inning with a spectacular off-balance throw from near the foul line in shallow left. In Game 2 he scored what would be the deciding run in a 6–5 win after he doubled with one out in the eighth inning. He led off Game 4 with a home run off righthander Bobby J. Jones, staking the Yankees to a lead they never lost in a 3–2 victory. He tied Game 5 at 2–2 in the sixth inning with a homer off lefty Al Leiter.

That game stayed even until the ninth. Leiter, working with two outs and two strikes on Jorge Posada, could not put him away. Posada fouled off two pitches, took a ball, fouled off another pitch, and took ball four on the ninth pitch of an at-bat that drained the last of Leiter's energy reserve. He'd thrown 138 pitches. He would never get that third out. Scott Brosius singled and then, on Leiter's 142nd pitch, so did Luis Sojo.

"A 15-hopper," Leiter lamented. The ball wiggled past Leiter and two diving infielders like a pedestrian crossing midtown traffic in the middle of a block. Posada slid home, and when the throw from centerfielder Jay Payton caromed off Posada's thigh and into the Mets' dugout, Brosius scored, too.

Jeter would make one more contribution. The denouement of the Series happened to be a clash of titans: righthander Mariano Rivera, the best reliever in postseason history, facing Mets slugger Mike Piazza with two outs and a runner on. Jeter called timeout and jogged to the mound. Shouting, he still had to press his mouth near Rivera's ear to be heard above the din of the crowd. "You know what he's trying to do here; he's trying to take you out," Jeter said forcefully. "Be smart. Don't be stupid. Don't just lay one over to try to get ahead. Be careful. This guy's not just trying to loop the ball over second. He wants to take you deep. Now let's go!"

Rivera got ahead with a called strike. Then Piazza swung and connected solidly with the next pitch, a belt-high fastball. With the scoreboard clock reading 12:00, it was literally the stroke of midnight. Torre screamed in the dugout, "No!" But a few steps from the warning track, the ball died an innocent death in the glove of centerfielder Bernie Williams. Jeter leaped into the arms of Sojo; he was a champion for a fourth time.

Two nights later Jeter rested his feet on an ottoman in his small, modestly furnished apartment on the East Side of Manhattan. His ironing board and iron stood at the ready by his dining table. He had slept past noon the past two days and left his apartment only for dinners, once in the Bronx with friends and this night in midtown with his parents. On Sunday he would eat downtown at a team party arranged by Torre. On Monday, after his fourth victory parade through lower Broadway, he was booked to do Letterman.

"No doubt, this team ranks up there with any team of all time," Jeter says. "You can come up with teams that had better players or hit more home runs or scored more runs. But the name of the game is winning. I can't see any team being better."

Outside, 11 floors below the drawn blinds, life after the Subway Series pulsed on. The usual cacophonous symphony of car horns and tire screeches continued. Nothing had changed. This winner wasn't going anywhere. More than ever, this is his town. More than ever, this is his team. ●

New York's shortstop
atop the dugout at
Yankee Stadium in 2000.

Excerpted from SPORTS ILLUSTRATED, August 13, 2001

Dear Derek…

Autograph requests, party invitations, and romantic proposals: all can be found amongst Derek Jeter's fan mail

BY RICK REILLY

The locker next to Derek Jeter's in the New York Yankees' home clubhouse throbs with his unopened mail. It piles up in feet. Spills onto the carpet. Gives off odd smells. Aches to be opened. So I asked him if I could open it all. He said yes. Here's what I found in 261 pieces of mail.

Despite pleas of URGENT! and IMPORTANT! and TAPE THIS ASAP TO DEREK JETER'S LOCKER! on the envelopes, most of the letter writers wanted only his autograph—141 to be exact, including 52 on Jeter photos they sent, 13 on baseballs they sent, the rest on all kinds of stuff, like a book report and a baby photo. To aid their cause, eight people even sent pens. One, seeking an autograph for her sailor husband, wrote, "Think of the publicity you'll get!" Tonight on the 11 o'clock news: Derek Jeter signs autograph for sailor!

Jeter is one of the rare athletes who tries to respond to all his mail himself, but he admitted, "I'm a couple road trips behind." It's no wonder. Reading his mail for one day is more depressing than watching the NASDAQ Composite. Most requests came from people who "wouldn't normally ask for something like this," except that they were hearing-impaired; had lost a grandfather, a best friend, or their appendix; had a brain tumor, an aneurysm, a breach baby, essential tremor disease, breast cancer, colitis, cerebral palsy, Down syndrome, or colon cancer; had gone through a rough divorce or fallen off a bike; were abandoned or unloved.

One hopelessly doomed woman needed an autograph because she had "lost four close friends, a father-in-law and almost an alcoholic father, had an apartment fire, had a miscarriage of twins, and has to take care of my loser husband." Lady, you don't need an autograph; you need a telethon.

There were three out-and-out come-ons from women, including one jaw-dropper that would make a dead man straighten his tie. She included her photo and her phone number "as a long shot that you might call me." Jeter wasn't going to. "I never date anybody that way," he said.

Jeter was sought out by fans both on the field and off.

Jeter was always a popular choice among autograph-seekers.

People really needed Jeter at their movie premieres (3), auctions (6), Playboy Mansion party, Eagle Scout ceremony, third-grade play, backyard BBQ ("and bring all your teammates"), boat ride, and birthday parties (3, including one in Tampa from a boy who wrote, "Make sure you bring your swimsuit").

There were four pitches from real estate agents—including a man who was standing by "for all your real estate needs in the greater Akron area"—and two people begging for money. One guy wanted $20,000. "That's only .002 of your income," he wrote, for "a small addition on our house…a car loan and… upgrading the musical equipment I have." Well, as long as it's an emergency!

Too bad Jeter doesn't have any money. Otherwise, why would MasterCard have sent a letter that read, "We regret to inform you that we are unable to approve your application at this time"? Jeter's average salary is only $19 million a year. Perhaps he should try for a debit card. Luckily, there was also a notice from an insurance group informing him that he might be "eligible for worker's comp benefits under Florida statute 440." Not only that, but he was entitled to "29 cents a mile" for doctors' visits.

It would mean "so, so much" if Jeter would accept people's gifts of bubble gum, poems (2), cookies (by the 100s), audio letters (2), shoes (wrong size), needlepoint, novels (2), rambling seven-page essays about Pokémon (6, all from the same woman), and a dead woman's favorite Yankees T-shirt and shorts, which, after three weeks in a plastic bag, stank to wherever she is now. "It was her final wish," wrote her daughter. "I'm hoping they bring you luck."

Nearly every request came with the phrase, "It'll only take a minute," except for the one from the kid who wanted Jeter to send a lot of baseball tips and the one from the mother who instructed Jeter to "write a brief, encouraging letter" to her Little Leaguer. What, no song?

Only nine people out of the 261 wanted nothing except to tell Jeter how much they loved watching him play ball. There was even a small, handwritten thank-you note—from David Letterman for appearing on his show.

Jeter had a game to play, so I asked him what he wanted me to do with it all. "Just stick it back in that locker," he said. I trucked the letters back in, only to find something awful sitting there.

The new mail. ●

Nearly every request came with the phrase, "It'll only take a minute," except for the one from the kid who wanted Jeter to send a lot of baseball tips and the one from the mother who instructed Jeter to "write a brief, encouraging letter" to her Little Leaguer. What, no song?

Jeter on deck in Seattle
in 2001.

Welcoming Bernie Williams back to the dugout after scoring a run in the 2001 ALDS against Oakland. The Yankees won the series in five.

Jeter rounds the bases in triumph after his game-winning home run in Game 4 of the 2001 World Series against Arizona. New York lost the series in seven.

Jeter's flair for the
dramatics...

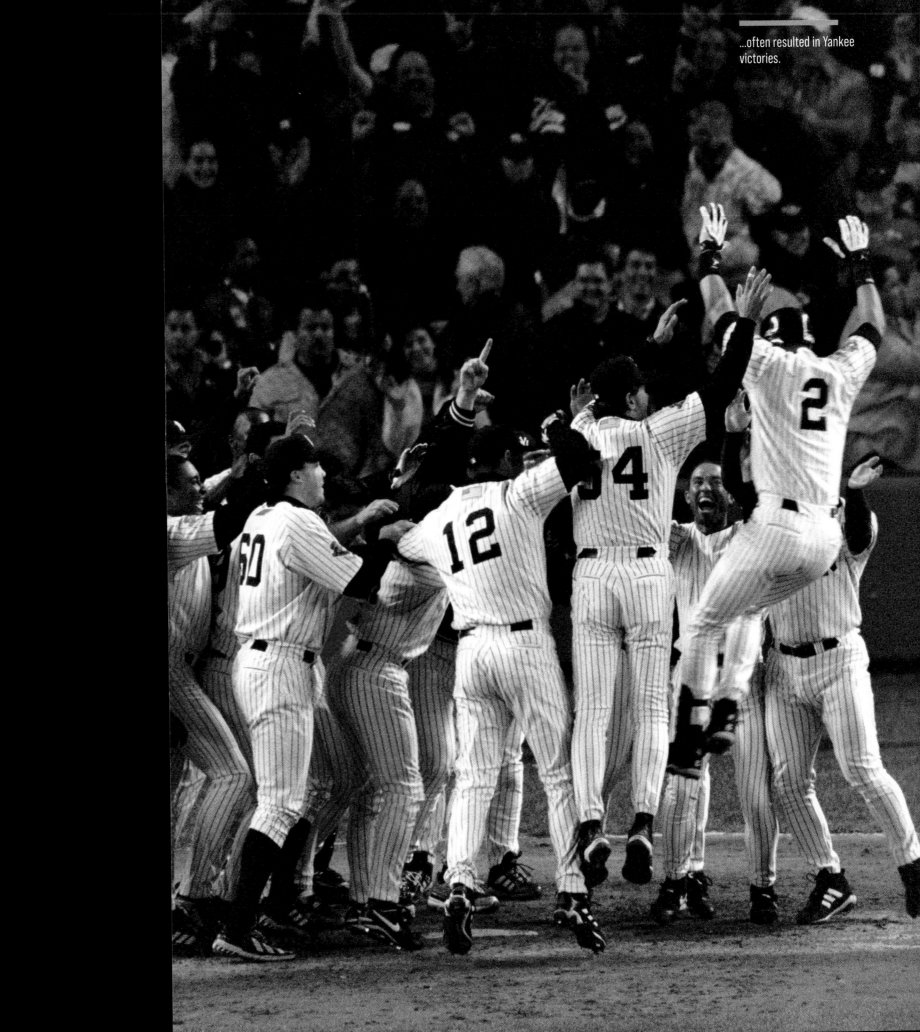

Waiting for his turn at the
plate in San Diego in 2002.

Making contact against
Seattle in 2002.

At-bat against the Marlins in the 2003 World Series, Jeter's fourth straight appearance in the Fall Classic.

A moment of levity against
the White Sox in 2004.

Excerpted from SPORTS ILLUSTRATED, June 7, 2004

Hitting Bottom

Even great hitters aren't immune to horrific slumps. How does a player like Derek Jeter suddenly lose his way at the plate—and how does he find his way back?

BY TOM VERDUCCI

A batting slump is baseball's version of the common cold. Sooner or later every hitter gets one, it can keep him up at night, and there is no known cure, though that does not prevent everyone and his doorman from passing on homemade remedies and get-well wishes.

Derek Jeter of the New York Yankees came down with a whopper of a case in April—he was 0-for-32 at its head-throbbing worst—that was so bad that he couldn't leave his Manhattan apartment without being reminded of it.

"The doorman would tell me, 'Tonight's the night! I've got a feeling this is it!'" Jeter says. "You're trying not to think about it, yet everywhere you go, you're constantly reminded of it. It wasn't so much people giving me advice as it was people saying, 'We're pulling for you.' It's everywhere you turn—people on the street, the questions from the media every day."

This season has produced even more proof that no one is immune. Career .300 hitters Jeter, Chipper Jones of the Atlanta Braves, and José Vidro of the Montreal Expos—who ranked seventh, 12th, and 18th, respectively, in career

batting average among active players entering this season—all were hitting worse than .250 at week's end. Fellow perennial All-Stars Carlos Delgado of the Toronto Blue Jays (.227), Bret Boone of the Seattle Mariners (.231), and Shawn Green of the Los Angeles Dodgers (.229) were similarly stricken. Welcome to the cold-and-flew-out-weakly-to-leftfield season.

"These guys are all proven hitters, and they're not old, either," Milwaukee Brewers general manager Doug Melvin says. "I think [at the end of the season] the numbers will be there. But some are digging such a big hole that they won't be able to put up the big numbers they have in the past."

Jones, for instance, had only two doubles and 13 RBIs at week's end, jeopardizing his streaks of five years with 30 doubles and eight

How the Lakers
CAN BE BEATEN
BY JACK McCALLUM

NBA FINALS

Shaquille
O'Neal

Sports Illustrated

THE SLUMP

SOLVING THE BIGGEST MYSTERY IN SPORTS

>>> **DEREK JETER** <<<
Career Batting Avg. .317
Avg. This Season Through May 25 .189
Avg. from May 26 to May 31 .458

years with 100 RBIs. Delgado, who suffered a sprained rib cage muscle while swinging against the Texas Rangers last Saturday, had eight homers and 32 RBIs, and was facing an uphill climb to continue his streak of six consecutive seasons with at least 33 homers and 102 RBIs.

For young hitters, a slump can infect an entire year, which is what happened last season to the Philadelphia Phillies' Pat Burrell (.209), the Cincinnati Reds' Adam Dunn (.215), and the Chicago White Sox's Paul Konerko (.234). Jeter, however, showed last week how stars with long track records of success can get well soon. Entering the Yankees' May 26 game against the Baltimore Orioles, Jeter, who hit .324 in 2003, was batting .189 after 190 at-bats. Suddenly, facing the Orioles and the Tampa Bay Devil Rays, he pounded out 11 hits in his next 24 at-bats, raising his average 31 points in five days, to .220. To hit .300 for the season—assuming he maintained his rate of at-bats—Jeter would need to hit .335 the rest of the way, not an unreasonable task for a career .317 hitter entering the season.

"I didn't see how people could be writing my obituary after one month," Jeter said last Saturday before hitting safely in his sixth straight game. "I knew all along there was a lot of the season left to play, so I wasn't concerned. It's frustrating when you're not getting your hits. I'm not going to lie to you about that. But you don't spend time thinking about what's already happened. You can't change it. You just look forward to the next game, especially when you know there are about 120 left."

Not coincidentally, the Yankees also began to look more like themselves last week, putting together their highest-scoring (61 runs) six-game winning streak in 46 years. After an 8–11 start during which they batted .217, the Yankees had the best record (30–19) and the most runs (275) in baseball—and their average was up to .265. "We feed off his energy, without a doubt," Yankees third baseman Alex Rodriguez says of shortstop Jeter. "He's a hitting machine.

A lot of good things happen when he gets going. He's the heartbeat of this team."

The slump—or at least its derivation in the English language—traces from the appropriately cold climes of Scandinavia and the Norwegian verb slumpa ("to fall"). In America a slumpa can take on many forms, though none as vivid as the one that falls at the beginning or end of a season and strikes a star player. Combine those elements, and you get historic droughts at the plate, such as the 0-for-21 suffered in the 1952 World Series by the Dodgers' Gil Hodges, whose slump the following season prompted Brooklyn priests to entreat their parishioners to pray for him; the 5-for-25 performance by the Boston Red Sox's Ted Williams in the 1946 World Series, which turned out to be his only postseason appearance; and Jeter's 0-for-32 run, which drew much more attention than the virtually simultaneous 0-for-37 skid by the Devil Rays' José Cruz Jr., a lifetime .251 hitter.

Bob Uecker, the former backup catcher, once said, "I had slumps that lasted into the winter." But with players such as Uecker, a career .200 hitter, it's hard to tell when a slump begins and ends. Likewise, pitcher Bob Buhl owns the worst 0-fer in major league history—0-for-88 over two seasons—but he was a career .089 hitter.

Dodgers infielder Robin Ventura went 0-for-41 as a rookie with the White Sox in 1990. Hall of Fame shortstop Luis Aparicio once endured an 0-for-44 slump. For position players, however, the sultan of slump is Bill Bergen, a Brooklyn catcher who went 0-for-46 in 1909 on his way to becoming the worst hitter of all time (minimum 1,000 at-bats), with a .170 batting average over 11 seasons. That an accomplished hitter such as Jeter could look like Bergen is testament to the humbling nature of baseball.

"Slumps are powerful things," says Rodriguez, who endured an 0-for-21 stretch with the Rangers in 2002. "Sometimes players are going so badly that, if they hit a pop-up near the third-base stands, they root for the ball to stay in play so the third baseman can catch it, just so they don't strike out again. I've heard of guys telling the catcher, 'Just tell me what pitch is coming because there's no way I'm getting a hit right now and I don't want to punch out again. Just let me put one ball in play.'"

Says Yankees DH Jason Giambi, "Oh, yeah, there are times you're going so bad you swing at the first pitch just so you don't get to another two-strike count, because you know you'll strike out. So you'll take your ground ball to second base and get out of there thinking, Okay, at least I made contact. That's something."

Slumps can be all-consuming, affecting a hitter's mood, appetite, and behavior. Former Yankees outfielder Paul O'Neill says that when he was in a slump, it "never really left me. It was what I thought about as I went to bed and the first thing when I got up in the morning."

Jeter was not immune to struggling at the plate during his illustrious career.

Says Devil Rays manager Lou Piniella, a former player notorious for his intensity, "When you're in a slump, thank God for the invention of the watercooler."

Slumps would awaken Piniella, a lifetime .291 hitter, in the middle of the night and, eventually, would rouse his wife too. Anita Piniella would hear yelling coming from downstairs and fear a burglar had entered the house. Instead she would find her frustrated husband swinging a bat in front of a mirror, talking to himself.

Hitting is an art with karmic overtones. Cold streaks are charged by the static of many disjointed thoughts. Hot streaks are marked by the absence of thought, or as the yogi Berra once philosophized, "How the hell are you going to think and hit at the same time?"

Like an artist visited by a muse, the hitter has an elusive relationship with the baseball goddess known as Feel. Explains Yankees centerfielder Bernie Williams, "You get the feeling that they can't get you out. It's something that seems to come from your inner being. You can't wait for your next at-bat. It's like riding a wave, being right in the middle of a 50-foot swell and riding it all the way in to shore, and then you paddle back out and do it as long as you can. And then [the feeling's] gone."

The loss of that feeling, however, can have practical explanations. As Jones says, "When I'm not hitting, 95 percent of the time it's something mechanical. So the key is to figure out what the mechanical flaw is. You get in the cage and try to work yourself out of it. The other five percent of the time, it's mental. Every time you go to the plate, you feel like they've got 12 people out on the field, there are no holes, and you're not going to get any hits."

Jeter's slump had mental and physical origins. As he pressed to get off to a good start, Jeter admits, his anxiety had him "jumping at the ball." Rather than waiting for a pitch to get to him, especially an outside pitch, Jeter would lean forward in his haste to hit it, jerking his head instead of keeping it steady. He was particularly hard-pressed to hit fastballs, which he had previously feasted on. Last year, for instance, he batted .330 against fastballs from righthanders on the outer third of the plate, according to the scouting service Inside Edge. In his first 43 games this year, however, Jeter was hitless in 16 at-bats decided by those same pitches. He struggled when hitting with two strikes (.127, versus .235 in 2003) and even when he was ahead in the count (.250, versus .459). Furthermore, his "well-hit average"—Inside Edge's category for hard-hit balls, regardless of

Says Jeter, "I never lose my confidence. It doesn't mean I'm going to get hits, but I have my confidence all the time."

whether they end up as base hits—dropped from .316 to .245.

"You're trying so hard to get hits instead of just hitting the ball," Jeter says. "But you can't guide the ball. Your eyes are the key. When your head moves, your eyes move, and you don't see the pitch as long. That's why when you're going good, the ball looks slower. You see it longer. Now I'm staying back, letting the ball get to me instead of trying to go out and get the ball."

Moreover, Jeter sometimes caught himself guessing the type and location of the next pitch. "I'm no good when I look for pitches," he says, "because if I look for something [and it comes close to that location], I'll swing no matter what. Like if I'm looking inside, the pitch could be about to hit me and I'll still swing at it."

Before his 0-for-32 slide, Jeter had never gone more than 18 at-bats without a hit. When he finally ended the slump with a leadoff home run against Barry Zito of the Oakland A's on April 29, he said after the game, "It's like a bad dream is over with." He added, "I wouldn't wish it on anybody." Not long thereafter, he fell into a 1-for-26 funk.

"[It] never really changed much," Giambi said about Jeter's demeanor, "and that's hard to do when it seems like nothing is going right. I remember in Boston he hit a couple of line drives to rightfield that would have been hits except Kevin Millar was playing a Little League right-field. When you're going bad, guys make plays on you that they're not supposed to make."

Says Jeter, "I never lose my confidence. It doesn't mean I'm going to get hits, but I have my confidence all the time."

According to New York manager Joe Torre, two of Jeter's three hits—flared doubles—in his breakout game against Baltimore were typical slump breakers. "All of a sudden you realize you don't have to hit it on the screws to get a hit," says Torre, a lifetime .297 hitter. Jeter added three hits in each of the next two games, after which Torre observed, "He looks very confident

up there now, and he's got an edge to him. His body language says, 'I know you're going to challenge me,' and he's up for it."

Says Piniella, who watched the Yankees shortstop go 5-for-15 last weekend against his Devil Rays, "Jeter can run, he hits the ball to all fields, and he can even bunt, so for a player like him to be in a prolonged slump is hard to imagine. But [it happens, and] it's humbling because you can't get away from it. It's on the talk shows, it's in the newspapers, it's on TV, and pretty soon it's larger than life. That's when I tell my guys, 'Look, your wife is still going to be there when you get home, your dog will still like you, and you'll still drive the same car. Just relax and hit the ball.'"

One AL scout says, "Slumps become worse when guys try to do too much. Boone is an example. He's trying to carry the club, and he's expanding his strike zone. He's swinging harder than I've ever seen him. He's not recognizing sliders away—he's just hacking up there. He's lost at the plate right now."

Stars such as Jeter, Delgado, Jones, Vidro, Boone, and Green still have more than two-thirds of the season left to approach their typical numbers. In 1941, for instance, Joe DiMaggio had been mired in one of the worst slumps of his career—a 20-game stretch over April and May in which he hit .184—when on May 15 he singled off White Sox lefthander Eddie Smith in the first inning. It was the start of his 56-game hitting streak, and he finished the year batting .357.

"People kept asking me if I was worried about Derek," Yankees GM Brian Cashman says. "My answer was always the same: no. Because if you look at late May every year, there are a couple of stars struggling to get out of the gate. And by the end of the year their numbers are there regardless. They've proven themselves over time, so you don't worry. It just happened to be Derek's turn this year. Next year? It'll be somebody else's turn." •

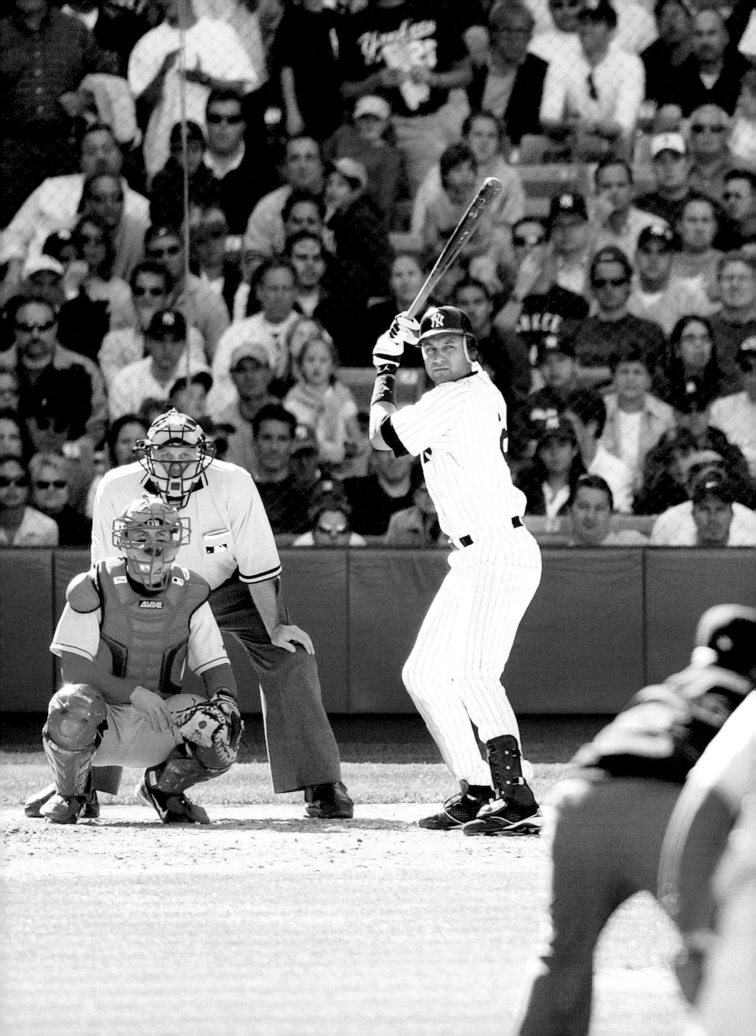

Awaiting a pitch against
the Red Sox in 2004.

The Dive: Jeter goes into the stands to catch a foul ball in the 12th inning against Boston in 2004. The Yankees won in 13 innings.

A casual Derek Jeter steering a boat in Tampa Bay in 2005.

Batting against Boston's David Wells
at Yankee Stadium in 2005.

Jeter and the Yankees hosted the Red Sox in the 2005 home opener.

In action against the
Rangers in 2005.

Excerpted from SPORTS ILLUSTRATED, August 19, 2009

Derek Jeter Underrated? Yankee Icon Great in a Tangible Way

*Though it is actually another invented word—Clemenate—that means: "To hate an athlete in an entirely healthy, fun sports way."

BY JOE POSNANSKI

The word, Jeterate, was born of my own frustration—a frustration shared with many people who are not in love with the Yankees—that Jeter (because of his looks, his charms, his charisma, his natural ability to lead, his pinstripes) will receive hosannas and standing ovations for more or less anything he does, even ridiculous stuff. Especially INTANGIBLES.

Oh, man. Don't get a Yankees fan started on Jeter's intangibles.

The breaking point for me came on a drive from Cooperstown to New York City when I had to endure an endless Jeter radio rhapsody after he got caught in a rundown between third and home. He was thrown out, of course, but apparently he stayed alive long enough to wave the other runners to the next base. The announcers made this bit of waving sound like the greatest bit of leadership in the world since Churchill talked about fighting them on the beaches. "How about that Derek Jeter! That's what makes him great!"

This has been constant. Jeter has received excessive praise for his defense—and three Gold Gloves—though various defensive statistics and subjective viewings suggested that he has been a subpar shortstop. (One of the longtime posters at the awesome "Baseball Think Factory" website gave himself the brilliant name "Pasta Diving Jeter"—a moniker so utterly inspired that I think it should be served at every restaurant in New York City.)

By 2009, Jeter had long since silenced any detractors.

Announcers and analysts of all kinds will write sonnets to Jeter's baseball brilliance—the guy never makes a mistake!—though a closer statistical view shows, for instance, he can be a spotty base runner (last year, for instance, Bill James' analysis showed Jeter to be minus-14 bases as a runner). Captain Clutch is actually hitting below his career averages with runners in scoring position, in late and close situations and in the postseason.

So, yes, I will admit that in the past Derek Jeter has inspired some—call it weariness, I guess. I've always thought he was a terrific player. And I've always thought he was overrated, too. That's a hard double to pull off.

But…now we'll get to the point of this story. I think that in many ways Derek Jeter this year has added a third title. He has, against all odds, become UNDERRATED. And that is a wicked turn. I think Jeter at 35 is having one of his greatest seasons. I think he's playing defense better than he ever has, he's getting on base and slugging like he did in his prime, and in my view he has been the Yankees' most valuable player in 2009. And, for once, it's funny, I don't hear too many other people talking about it.

Now, let me be clear—there is absolutely no doubt in my mind that the American League MVP this year is Minnesota's Joe Mauer, and nobody else is even close, and I feel so strongly about this that I am doing daily updates about it on my blog. But the Twins are probably not going to make the playoffs, and there are many people who feel that the most valuable player must come from a playoff team. And if that's the case then… well, I think at this moment Jeter might be my MVP, non-Mauer division.

Look: he's hitting .330 through Tuesday and has a .394 on-base percentage—tied with A-Rod for best on the Yankees. He's on pace for 218 hits, 109 runs, 21 homers, 27 stolen bases. He's having a great offensive season, quite similar to the season last year's MVP, Boston's Dustin Pedroia, had.

And—this is weird—those advanced statistics that have so universally mocked his defense now show him to be, well, darned good defensively. The Dewan Plus/Minus system—a video system where they plot every ball hit in play—had long shown him to consistently be the worst shortstop in baseball. Now, it has him as a plus-7 shortstop, a top-10 shortstop. Ultimate Zone Rating—UZR—which had shown him to be costing his team runs defensively every single year since 2002 now calculates that he has saved the Yankees almost six runs this year. Jeter has made it clear he doesn't care about such statistics, so it probably gives him no satisfaction.

Still, the numbers suggest that he's playing shortstop better than he has in years. Two baseball insiders concur, saying that he positions himself better now than he ever did before and his already quick release has gotten even quicker. Plainly, not as many grounders are getting past a diving Jeter.

This is a good time to consider the Jeter career. This week, he passed Luis Aparicio and became the all-time hit leader for shortstops. It was a nice moment, though Jeter has really been nothing at all like Aparicio—a brilliant defensive shortstop who did not get on base but still led off for most of his career because he was fast (he led the league in stolen bases every year from 1956–64).

Truth is, there has not really been a shortstop who compares all that well to Jeter since World War II. Well, there's Alex Rodriguez—but he has been a third baseman for the last six years and probably won't ever play shortstop again. There's Hall of Famer Robin Yount, though he really had some of his best offensive seasons as a centerfielder. There's Barry Larkin, who was a superb blend of power, speed, and defense.

But Jeter is the only lifelong shortstop to hit 200 homers and steal 200 bases. He's the only lifelong shortstop the last 60 years to punch up an on-base percentage better than .375 (.387 lifetime—and on-base percentage is probably the most telling single offensive stat). He's moving into the top 50 lifetime in runs scored—and there's every reason to believe that by the end of his career he will be in the top 10, maybe even the top five if he plays well into his 40s.

And hits? Well, the Hit King Pete Rose had 2,762 hits on the day he turned 36. Jeter, assuming health, will have more when he turns 36 next June.

"Tell Derek that the first 3,000 hits are easy," Rose said, and it's a good line, but the truth is that Jeter should breeze past 3,000 hits and, depending on how important it is to him, could really climb the charts if he wants to keep going and going.

And that's probably the most compelling part of the Derek Jeter story now. He really could keep going and going. While it is true that he has always been admired in and around New York—worshipped even—the truth is that the last couple of years there have been increasingly louder whispers that his end is nigh. Even two or three years ago, people around New York already began to worry about what would happen when Jeter's contract ran out after the 2010 season. Would the Yankees have to overpay to keep him in his twilight years? Would he insist on staying at shortstop even if his usefulness there had run out? Would he continue to lead off after he stopped getting on base? Or (gasp) would he actually leave New York—and could you even imagine Derek Jeter wearing a uniform other than the Yankees' pinstripes?

The worry became palpable last year. For the first time, Jeter really did look old. He was hitting .270 in mid-June last year and he wasn't hitting with any power and the Yankees were struggling and there was this sense that the Jeter story was unhappily winding down.

But, turns out, the obits were premature. Jeter is still Jeter. He hit his usual .323/.390/.430

the rest of the way in 2008, and this year he has been preposterously consistent. Batting average isn't a great measuring tool, but it's telling that Jeter is hitting at home (.319) and on the road (.340), in wins (.337) and losses (.318), with men on base (.315) and with nobody on base (.339). He crushes lefties (.429), and he's hit well in short at-bats (.403 when putting the first pitch in play) and long at-bats (.480 when the at-bat is seven pitches or more).

I throw all these rather pointless numbers out there because Jeter's greatness as a player so often gets packaged inside the "intangibles" box. He's a leader! He's a winner! He has incredible instincts! He's always in the right place at the right time! He never makes a mental mistake! Every time he makes a smart play—he does make a lot of smart plays, good players do that—the Jeter as Saint thing grows, making a lot of baseball fans across America want to gag.

And it's those sorts of things that have led many to consider Jeter a media creation. Well, he's not. He's a great player having another great season. He's one of the best hitting shortstops in baseball history. He's an absolute first ballot Hall of Famer even if his career ended tomorrow.

And in my mind, if Yankees fans want to push one of their own as an MVP candidate they should stop pushing first baseman Mark Teixeira. He's hitting well, but he's a first baseman and they're supposed to hit. Tex is having roughly the same sort of offensive season that other American League first basemen are having. Put his numbers into a pile with Detroit's Miguel Cabrera, Boston's Kevin Youkilis, Minnesota's Justin Morneau, and even the Angels' Kendrys Morales—there isn't much separating them.

Instead push the Captain, Mr. November, the best-hitting shortstop in the long history of the New York Yankees. Jeter is great, and he is unique, and it's not about intangibles. No. That's the point. It's tangible. ●

Celebrating with Alex Rodriguez during Game 4 of the 2009 ALCS against the Angels.

Excerpted from Sports Illustrated, December 7, 2009

2009 Sportsman of the Year

It is not so much what he accomplished at 35—a fifth World Series ring capping a historic season, to be sure— as how the Yankees' shortstop arrived at his iconic place. Being the ultimate team player and a role model synonymous with winning has brought him still another title

BY TOM VERDUCCI

Every sunrise is a fresh shot at victory for Derek Jeter. Every day is an invitation to compete with the same smile and delight of that boy in the mirror who looked back at him on the eve of Little League Opening Day in Kalamazoo, Mich.

Young Derek would gaze upon himself for the first time in his new jersey—a T-shirt actually, with a sponsor's silk-screened name, such as D.M. BROWN CO.—then race to show his mom, Dorothy, and his dad, Charles. There would be a parade the next day, each kid in his new shirt marching a few blocks to the Little League field. A quarter century later Dr. Charles Jeter can close his eyes and still see his boy walking in Kalamazoo, "smiling…his chest is out…looks like his mom."

There is something even better now, though. Charles can open his eyes wide and see that same boy playing shortstop for the New York Yankees. "I still see that same joy," Charles says.

The need to win for Derek Sanderson Jeter knows neither rest nor discretion. Whether he is pulling a prank or a base hit, he pursues victory with the Shakespearean conviction that "things won are done; joy's soul lies in the doing."

This was a very good year for the soul of the Yankees' shortstop, whose pursuit of victory crested anew at 11 minutes to midnight on Nov. 4, when he became a World Series champion for the fifth time. After the Yankees closed out the Phillies in six games, the players, executives, trainers, batboys, friends, girlfriends,

DOUBLE ISSUE

SPORTSMAN *of the* YEAR

Sports Illustrated

SI.COM

Yankees Shortstop
DEREK JETER

161 Street-
Yankee Stadium
Station

B D 4

161 St & River Av NE

DECEMBER 7, 2009

family members, and hangers-on filled almost all 3,344 square feet of the team's celebratory clubhouse. Charles and Dorothy Jeter, however, were nowhere to be found. They have been in the Yankees' clubhouse only once, back in 1995, when Jeter first reached the big leagues, and even then they had to be coaxed in by one of his teammates and stayed only briefly.

"They think, This is where you work. They don't want to get in the way," Jeter explains, "but you still want to share it with them."

So Jeter stepped outside the clubhouse into a service concourse, where Dorothy and Charles stood. Each hugged their son and told him how proud they were of him. "Thank you," he told them.

It had been nine years since New York won the world championship. Jeter was just 26 years old then, the young prince of the city. Now he is 35, coming off perhaps the most impressive of his 15 big league seasons, bearing the patina of a man in full. Last summer, as their son chased the franchise record for hits, held by Lou Gehrig, Dorothy and Charles told Derek to take time to savor what was unfolding. "I'm always moving on to what's next," Derek says, "so they make it a point to tell me to appreciate things as you experience them."

"I think I was speaking to him when I told him that, but I was also speaking to myself," Charles says. "I've been very proud of him, on and off the field. He's a grown man now. The way he's grown up…this year has had me reflecting."

Two days after winning the Series the Yankees were honored with a parade through the Canyon of Heroes in Lower Manhattan. Most of the Yankees were flanked by wives, girlfriends, children, or celebrities. Jeter rode along Broadway on a float with his mom, dad, and sister, Sharlee. "I pretty much said, 'You're coming on the float, right?'" says Jeter, who was also joined by his girlfriend, actress Minka Kelly. "And they said, 'Yeah, we'd like

to.' I always like sharing things with my family. They're the reason why I'm here. They're as much a part of it as I am."

The good son loved the parade. He was smiling the whole time, his chest out.

It was a year in full for Jeter. In addition to winning his fifth World Series and breaking Gehrig's team record for hits (and Hall of Famer Luis Aparicio's record for hits by a shortstop), he won his fourth Gold Glove, his fourth Silver Slugger as the premier hitting shortstop in the league, the Roberto Clemente Award for his humanitarian service, and the Hank Aaron Award as the fans' choice for the best hitter in the American League.

Jeter batted .334—among shortstops in the last 100 years, only Honus Wagner has hit higher after turning 35—and accumulated 200 hits and 30 stolen bases for the third time; no other shortstop of any age has reached those standards more than once. He hit .407 in the World Series, playing his best baseball at the end of a 10-month, 190-game odyssey that spanned the World Baseball Classic, spring training, the regular season, and three rounds of the postseason. Jeter captained the U.S. team in the WBC, after which commissioner Bud Selig sent him a letter of thanks in which he called him "Major League Baseball's foremost champion and ambassador."

"You embody all the best of Major League Baseball," Selig wrote in the March 30 letter. "As I mentioned to you in our recent telephone conversation, you have represented the sport magnificently throughout your Hall of Fame career. On and off the field, you are a man of great integrity, and you have my admiration."

For those achievements, but most especially for the principled, selfless manner in which he earned them, Jeter is Sports Illustrated's 2009 Sportsman of the Year. He is the first Yankee to win the award in its 56-year history and only the third baseball player in the past 34 years to win the award alone, joining Orel Hershiser (1988) and Cal Ripken Jr. (1995).

Jeter is an anachronism if you believe that manners and humility, the pillars of sportsmanship, are losing ground in an increasingly stat-obsessed, self-absorbed sporting culture in which the simple act of making a tackle, dunking a basketball, or getting a base hit calls for some burlesque act of celebration, a marking of territory for individual purpose. Jeter is the unadorned star, and not only in the literal sense in that he is free of tattoos, piercings, cussing, and the other clichés of the big-time-jock starter kit. The actress Kim Basinger once captured the essence of Jeter as well as any scout, telling SI in 1999, "He's a hunk, and I don't even like that word. Women like guys who have a big presence but sort of play it down. It's very appealing."

Such uncalculating humility, alloyed to his formidable skills, is the same attribute that makes Jeter so appealing to teammates and foes alike. There is a natural fluidity to the way Jeter moves about, on the job and off, that puts people at ease. Even at 18, when the Yankees sent him to Instructional League to work on his fielding, Jeter had the ability to establish himself as an alpha male in a pack of ballplayers without having to be muscular about it.

"Right away the players gravitated toward him," says Brian Butterfield, his instructor then and now a Blue Jays coach. "He was well-liked, had a great disposition, a good sense of humor and a smile on his face, but when it got to working, that grin would melt into a serious look. He also had the best aptitude I've been blessed to be around. The stuff we worked on, he picked up so quickly."

Jeter's rare gift as a superstar athlete is that he doesn't so much inspire awe as he engenders comfort. To be around Jeter is to truly believe that things are going to turn out well, whether you are a fan who still wants to believe in the inspirational quality of sports and the people who play them, or a Yankee who wants to believe there is some way back from three runs down, five outs from elimination, against Pedro Martínez in his prime.

"Everything he does has such a grace about it," A's general manager Billy Beane says. "Even now, this last postseason, people would say to me, 'You must be rooting against the Yankees.' But you know, maybe because of Jeter, the Yankees know how to win. It's not an act. The Yankees' brand name in this era is that it is Jeter's era. It's similar to what DiMaggio was in his era."

Eight years ago, to his recollection, Beane watched Jeter run out a routine ground ball to shortstop in the late innings of a routine game in which the Athletics were beating the Yankees. Jeter ran down the first base line in 4.1 seconds, a time only possible with an all-out effort. Beane was so impressed by the sprint that he ordered his staff to show the video of that play to all of the organization's players in spring training the following year.

"Here you have one of the best players in the game," Beane says, "who already had made his money and had his four championships by then, and he's down three runs in the seventh inning running like that. It was a way of showing our guys, 'You think you're running hard, until you see a champion and a Hall of Famer run.' It wasn't that our guys were dogging it, but this is different. If Derek Jeter can run all out all the time, everybody else better personally ask themselves why they can't."

Told the story, Jeter says, "It makes you feel good whenever anybody appreciates how you do things. My whole thing is, you're only playing for three hours a day. The least you can do is play hard. You have what, four or five at-bats? Okay, it's not difficult to run, to give it a hundred percent. It's effort. You don't have to have talent for effort."

The idea of Jeter as a template stretches beyond 90 feet. He is a role model not only

DEREK JETER

for how to play baseball but also for how to remain atop the wobbly pedestal of fame. DiMaggio never swam in the dangerous currents Jeter has known. Jeter has played through the Steroid era, through 15 seasons

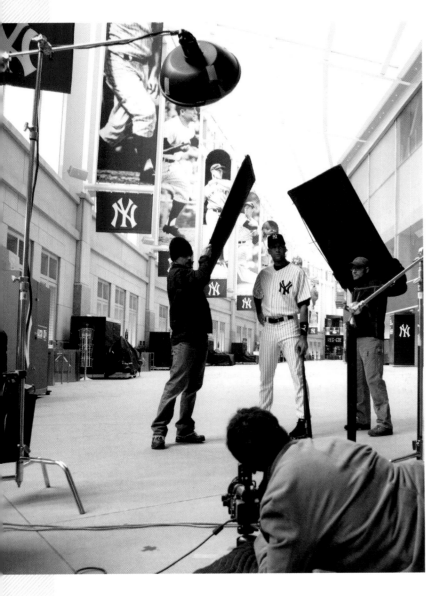

Behind the scenes at the 2009 Sportsman of the Year photo shoot.

under the watch of the New York tabloids and through the rise of the Internet, bloggers, and cellphone cameras and made it through, as far as notoriety goes, untainted in that way as well. When Jeter broke Gehrig's franchise hits record, against the Orioles on Sept. 11, former All-Star righthander Curt Schilling wrote in his blog, "Derek Jeter has always been above the fray. As someone who's wallowed in it, 'foot-in-mouthed' it hundreds of times, said dumb things and backed up dumber ones, it's refreshing. He's shown up, played and turned in a first-ballot Hall of Fame career in the hardest environment in sports to do any/all of the above…. I know competing against that guy, for the decade or so we matched up, was what made the major leagues the major leagues for someone like me."

How has he done it? Jeter was thrown into the Gotham maw at the age of 21, less than four years removed from his graduation from Kalamazoo Central High, but even then he understood the navigational charts of fame, the big city, and success. Former teammate David Cone says that for months during that 1996 season, Yankees veterans would look for any of the typical openings to jump on a rookie—the way he dressed, the quotes he gave reporters, "anything," Cone says—but found nothing. They finally gave up. By the second half of Jeter's rookie season his teammates stopped looking for a reason to humble him and started looking to him to lead them.

It was during that season that Jeter told his father in a hotel room in Detroit while sharing a pizza, "Dad, I want to start a foundation to help kids."

"There are a lot of ways you can give back," replied Charles, a substance-abuse counselor who has a Ph.D. in sociology. "If you want to start a foundation, you've got to put in a lot of work. You can give back without a foundation."

"No, this is what I want to do," Derek said, "and I want you to help."

That year Jeter established the Turn 2 Foundation to create and support programs in western Michigan, New York City, and Tampa, where he lives in the off-season, to help young people live a drug- and alcohol-free lifestyle. "I thought maybe we could raise fifty-, a hundred-thousand dollars," Jeter says. The foundation raised $300,000 in its first year. Since then it has awarded more than $10 million in grants, including $500,000 recently to launch the Derek Jeter Academy in Tampa, an outpatient counseling center for teens seeking individual or family substance-abuse treatment. The foundation is run principally by Charles, Dorothy, Sharlee, and Derek.

If you imagined a man's life as an ever-growing ball of string, with his experiences and attributes represented by thousands of strands gathered along the way, virtually any string you pull in the life of Derek Jeter leads you back to his parents, the white daughter of a New Jersey church handyman and the Black son of a single mother in Alabama. It is because of the lessons of Dorothy and Charles that Derek is the rare star athlete known as much for who he is as for what he has done.

Dorothy, an accountant, and Charles met in Germany, where both were serving in the Army. Upon returning to the U.S., the couple settled in New Jersey, where Derek and Sharlee were born, before moving to Kalamazoo when Charles enrolled at Western Michigan University to pursue his master's degree. Dorothy and Charles required Derek and Sharlee to sign a commitment every August regarding rules of behavior, such as avoiding alcohol and drugs and respecting others.

"He was brought up to respect his environment and respect himself," Dorothy says. "When you like who you are, you're going to respect others. It's very simple."

"You've got to have strong values because there are people who don't want to see you attain or achieve," Charles says. "I don't think you magically get those values when you're successful. If you don't have it by then, you're going to be in a lot of trouble."

"I would be the same person regardless of what I was doing or where I was playing," says Jeter, who still talks to his parents each day. "It's not like I'm trying to act a certain way to make people happy. I'm just who I am. But again, it's something that I learned at a young age."

The first time Jeter found himself one win away from his fifth world championship was on Nov. 3, 2001, in Game 6 of the World Series against the Arizona Diamondbacks. The night went horribly wrong for the Yankees, to the point that manager Joe Torre, with his team losing 15–0, pulled Jeter, catcher Jorge Posada, and first baseman Tino Martinez from the game in the fifth inning as an act of surrender. Jeter walked into the clubhouse to change out of his spikes and into a pair of more comfortable turf shoes. In the training room he saw Jay Witasick, a journeyman reliever for the Yankees who in 1⅓ innings had given up nine runs, eight of them earned, a Series record for a reliever. As Jeter walked by, he heard Witasick say, "Well, at least I had fun."

"Derek just jumped all over him," Posada says. "Derek couldn't believe what he was saying. He was really, really hot. That was the angriest I've ever seen him."

Last week, sitting in an airport hangar in Long Beach, Calif., surrounded by a small army of people to shoot a commercial for Gillette, Jeter nodded when he was asked about the episode with Witasick. "I remember," Jeter said. Slowly, he began to get agitated again. "Fun? I can't relate to it. I really can't relate to it. I'll never forget that. At least you had fun? I'll never understand it. I don't want to understand it."

Anger is an emotion Jeter rarely displays. "Oh, yeah," he continued. "Everybody gets angry. What makes me angry is when people don't care—not when they fail; everybody fails—or when people act like they don't care. You have one opportunity to do something, and you never know if you're going to get that opportunity again."

After that night's loss to Arizona, and a 3–2 defeat in Game 7 one night later, it took Jeter and the Yankees eight more years to get it right, to win the last game of the baseball season, which is the only way Jeter defines a successful season. "I forgot how good it felt," he says. "We've been in the playoffs every year except 2008, and every year you think you have a chance. Then when you lose, it's so hard. I think it should be hard on everyone. I don't know if everyone feels the same way I do, but you put in all that time and work and effort to win a championship, and then you lose? You don't ever forget that feeling."

Every all-time great ballplayer establishes a brand, a shorthand identifier that captures what makes him iconic. For Ruth, for instance, it was the home run. Mays was a thrilling body in motion, Aaron represented strength of character, Mantle a comic-book heroism, Koufax the curveball, Ryan the fastball, Rose all-out hustle, and Reggie the month of October. Jeter is unique this way. He has forged an identity as the ultimate team player in a team sport.

Of the 2,138 regular-season games Jeter has played in his major league career, only one was meaningless—that is, a game in which the Yankees had been mathematically eliminated from a shot at the postseason and the subsequent possibility of winning the World Series. He has won 60.3% of the games in which he has played, the highest percentage among active players who have appeared in at least 1,000 games.

Pull on this thread, this need of his to win, and of course it takes you back to his parents. Derek attended afternoon kindergarten. He knew it was time for school when *The Price Is Right* ended. He watched the show with his father. They would bid against each other while playing along with the show's finale, the showcase showdown. "He never let me win," Jeter says. "He never let me win anything, checkers or whatever."

Kalamazoo has given the world Shakespeare fishing rods, Gibson guitars, Checker cabs, and Jeter's will to win, in that order of rigidity. If you were to draw up a list of Jeter's dislikes, most all of them would be what he regards as obstacles to winning:

1. Individuals who don't care about winning.

2. Self-promoters. "I never liked people who talked about themselves all the time, gloat," he says. "If you're accomplished and have done things, people will talk about it for you. I don't think you have to point it out. I'm not judging anybody. That's just the way I am."

3. Measuring success by individual statistics. "In this day and age, not just in baseball but in sports in general, all people care about is stats, stats, stats," he says. "You've got fantasy this, fantasy that, where you pay attention to stats. But there are ways to win games that you don't get a stat for."

4. Injury talk. "You either play or you don't play. If you're playing, nobody wants to know what's bothering you. Sometimes it's a built-in excuse for failing."

5. Negativity. Jeter wants nothing to do with negative questions from reporters or negative talk from teammates. He once went 0-for-32 and refused to admit he was in a slump. "We weren't allowed to use the word can't—'I can't do this, can't do that,'" Jeter says of his childhood. "My mom would say, 'What? No.' She's always positive. I don't like people always talking about the negative, negative, negative, because once you get caught in that mind-set, it's hard to get out of it."

Last week, the day after the commercial shoot with Gillette, Jeter did a Gatorade spot at Angels Stadium. As Jeter and Jack Tiernan, one of his agents at the Creative Artists Agency, walked toward an SUV for their ride to the

"If you're accomplished," Jeter says, "people will talk about it for you. You don't have to point it out."

stadium, Jeter snickered at a stretch limo parked next to the SUV. "Somebody going to the prom?" he joked. As Jeter went to enter the SUV, its driver waved him off, pointed to the limo, and said, "That's yours." Jeter was disappointed. The transportation company had tried too hard.

Watching Jeter shoot a commercial is like watching him play for the Yankees: he exudes a down-to-earth charm and boyish enthusiasm that make him a star without acting like one, but he is out to win. "One moment he can be joking with somebody in the stands while on deck," says Casey Close, his primary agent, "asking them, 'What do you think they're going to throw me here?' And then it's like with a snap of his fingers, he gets lost in the moment of the at-bat and his focus is incredible. One of the most impressive things about him is a calm sense of self, a complete confidence in exactly who he is."

"I don't think I've changed," Jeter says. "I think people around you change. The way they react when you're around. My closest friends I've had for a long time." His inner circle is small, populated by friends he met before he got to the big leagues, including teammates Posada, Mariano Rivera, and Andy Pettitte;

two longtime friends, Douglas Biro and Sean Twitty; and former teammate Gerald Williams, who Jeter says "always looked out for me" in his first major league training camp (1993) and who lives near him in Tampa.

"There are a few reasons why teammates look to Derek and respond to him," Posada says. "He doesn't make any excuses—about anything—and whenever he hears anything negative, he's going to prove you wrong. That fuels him to get better."

For the Gatorade commercial, Jeter was shot in super-slow-motion high definition by a camera moving along a track as he made his trademark jump throw, a leaping throw to first base deep from the shortstop hole. The shot was spectacular to the point of artistry, a kind of Baryshnikov meets *The Matrix*. "It's almost perfect," gushed the young, enthusiastic director, Adam Berg. Almost. The director tried more takes. Jeter finally presented Berg with a proposal.

"I told you I would do five jumps and three slides," Jeter said, referring to another scene in which he slid into second base. "But I'll make you a deal: I'll do 10 jumps and six slides, and all you have to do is swallow one spoonful of cinnamon. If not, five and three. Just one spoonful."

"With water?" Berg asked.

"Only after you swallow it."

Jeter's jump throw ranks with the basket catch of Willie Mays as one of the signature plays in baseball history. Still, Jeter's defense, especially his range, has been an object of derision by statistical analysts. "There is no possible way you can measure it," Jeter says of defensive skill, which he said includes too many variables that cannot be quantified. "There's just no way. It's impossible. Everybody is entitled to their opinion, but…no way."

After the 2007 season, at 33, Jeter hired a personal trainer, Jason Riley, to improve his leg strength and agility. As a young player Jeter didn't work out at all in November and December. "What I found out as you get older," he says, "is it's a lot easier to stay in shape than get back into shape." He worked with Riley throughout the winter, waking at 5:30 a.m. to finish by 7:30, even before spring training workouts. He worked with Riley again last winter. The results became obvious this year, when Jeter pleased even the statistical analysts with his improved range and footwork.

And he showed no evidence of decline at the plate. Only three shortstops have hit .300 in the season in which they were 36 or older, but Jeter appears to have the staying power to join them. Indeed, Jeter, with roughly the same number of hits (2,747) as Pete Rose had at 35, could join Rose and Ty Cobb as the only players to reach 4,000 hits if he plays through his early 40s, and perhaps he will even challenge Rose's record 4,256.

"I want to play as long as I'm having fun," Jeter says. "If I'm not having fun, I'm not going to be out there just to be out there. Right now I'm having as much fun as I've had since Little League. People say, 'How long do you want to play short?' I don't think about where I'll be playing six years down the road. I don't

see any reason why I can't play it for a long time."

Somebody fetched a plastic spoon and a jar of cinnamon. Jeter allowed Berg to examine them, then loaded the spoon with the spice, doing his level best to maintain an air of seriousness. He had arranged similar wagers earlier this year with teammate Brian Bruney and then one of the clubhouse attendants, not to be confused with his other favorite wager that involves asking someone if they think they can eat five saltines in one minute. Berg couldn't believe his luck; all he had to do was swallow the cinnamon and Jeter would have to give him 10 takes toward getting the perfect jump-throw shot.

As soon as Berg shoved the spoon in his mouth, Jeter jumped away laughing. Quickly, Berg gagged, his cheeks puffed, his eyes watered, and cinnamon smoke began spewing from a crack in his pursed lips. He looked like a man about to burst. Berg grabbed a bottle of water and began gulping from it.

"That's it!" Jeter shouted. "You lose! The deal was no water until you swallowed it."

After several minutes to recover, Berg asked Tiernan, "He's not serious, is he?"

"Oh, he's serious," Tiernan replied.

Another victory, however small, for Derek Jeter, today's superstar most synonymous with winning. But none of the accoutrements of his success—the five rings, the $189 million contract, the national endorsements, and the starlet on his arm—capture the essence of his success. In the difficult days of the Philippines campaign during World War II, General Douglas MacArthur wrote "A Father's Prayer," which begins, "Build me a son, O Lord." MacArthur prayed for a son with, among other traits, "humility, so that he may always remember the simplicity of true greatness." Therein lies true victory. The great wonder is not that Jeter has won so much but that he has won so well. He is the good son, the good winner. ●

"I want to thank the Good Lord for making me a Yankee" *DiMaggio ER 1949*

Jeter never tired of walking to the field and under a sign inscribed with a quote from Joe DiMaggio.

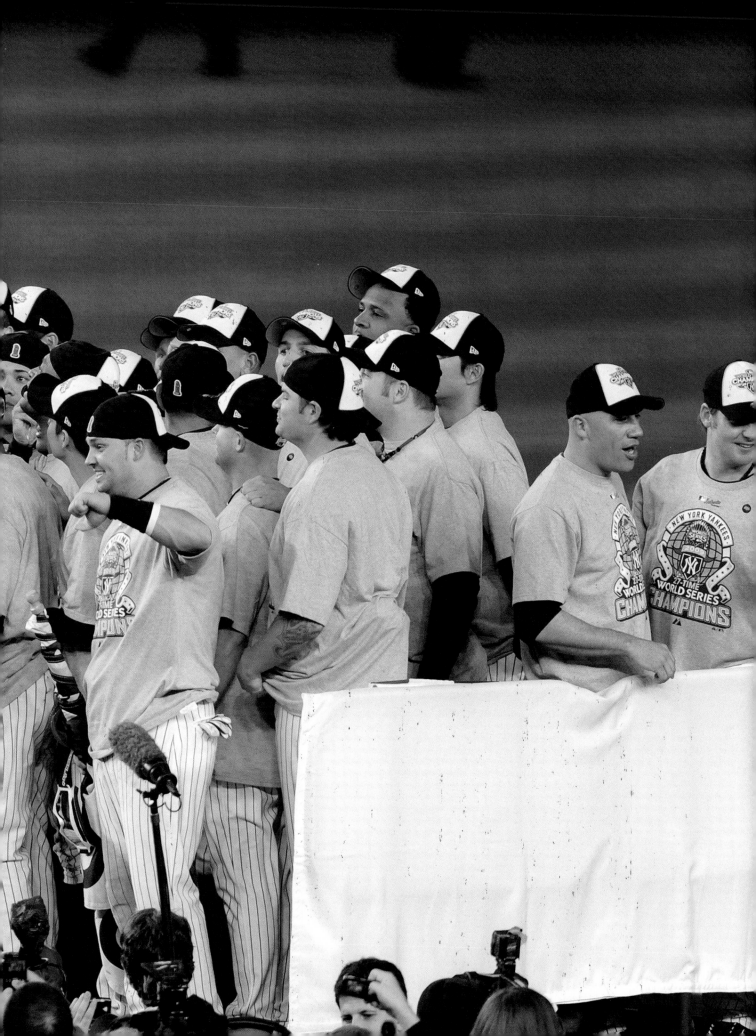

A classic jump throw
in Fenway Park in 2010.

Jeter ranges to his left for a ball against the Angels in 2010.

A YANKEE LEGEND

During the second game of a doubleheader against Boston in 2012.

2010–2013

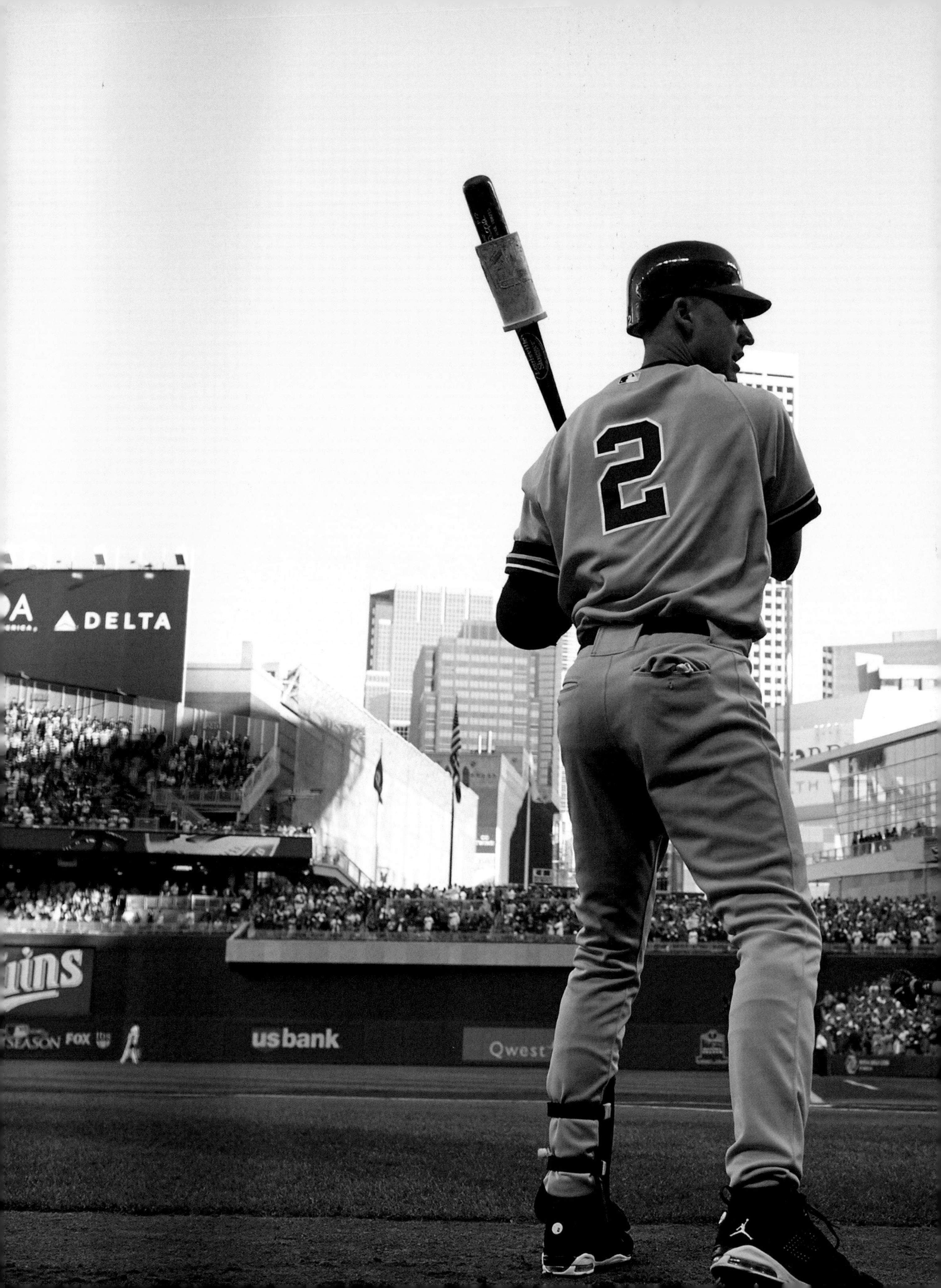
DELTA
usbank
Qwest

Jeter is on deck during Game 2 of the 2010 ALDS in Minnesota.

On base during Game 2 of the
2010 ALCS against the Angels.

Excerpted from SPORTS ILLUSTRATED, May 3, 2010

So Far, So Good

The Core Four, heart of the Yankees' dynasty, look back on their friendships and careers over lunch

BY TOM VERDUCCI

Beginning in February 1990, the Yankees signed Mariano Rivera, Jorge Posada, Andy Pettitte, and Derek Jeter within 28 months of one another. All four made their big league debuts in 1995, and except for the three seasons when Pettitte played for his hometown Astros (2004–06), they have been together ever since, sharing championships and life's milestones, big and small, like brothers.

The Core Four—Rivera is 40; Posada, 38; Pettitte, 37; and Jeter, 35—have combined for 27 All-Star selections, 11 division titles, seven American League pennants, five world championships, and $562 million in career earnings. In accomplishment and longevity, the sports world has seen nothing quite like this quartet. This year Rivera, Posada, and Jeter became the first trio of teammates in any North American sport to stay together for 16 consecutive seasons. And there is no indication that any of the four, fresh off winning World Series ring number five in 2009, is close to being finished. Rivera (six saves, 0.00 ERA through Sunday), Posada (.315 batting average), Jeter (.316), and Pettitte (3–0, 1.29) helped the Yankees win their first five series of the season—the first Yankees team to do so since 1926.

Mo, Sado, Andy, and Jeet, as they call one another, have spent more of their adulthood with one another than their own families. (Since they first met, all but Jeter have become husbands and fathers; Jeter was the best man at Posada's wedding.) One finishes another's sentences, they can communicate with just a look, and they operate a kind of elder's tribunal in the New York clubhouse. They also have built virtually spotless reputations, save for when Pettitte admitted in 2007 to twice using human growth hormone. When he faced questions from reporters about his transgression, Rivera, Posada, and Jeter were, of course, near his side.

In all those years, however, Rivera, Posada, Pettitte, and Jeter had never shared a meal except as part of larger groups—until SI gathered the Core Four for lunch last week at the St. Regis Hotel

The World's Bravest Athlete
by GARY SMITH

College Football Earthquake
by AUSTIN MURPHY

NBA PLAYOFFS
WHERE THE WILD THINGS ARE PAGE 32

Sports Illustrated

SI.COM

MAY 3, 2010

THE CORE FOUR

THE HEART OF THE YANKEES' DYNASTY BROKE IN TOGETHER 16 SEASONS AGO. IT'S ABOUT TIME THEY DID LUNCH

By TOM VERDUCCI

PAGE 38

"TAKE A PICTURE. YOU WON'T SEE THIS AGAIN. IN ANY SPORT."
— Mariano Rivera (second from right), posing with Derek Jeter, Jorge Posada and Andy Pettitte

in San Francisco, for a discussion moderated by senior writer Tom Verducci. Rivera, the closer, was the first one to show—two minutes early. Asked to predict who'd be the last to arrive, Rivera said, "Sado. Jeter, then Sado will be last."

Pettitte, the starting pitcher, arrived next, and then, just as Rivera was lecturing on punctuality and half-jokingly threatening to leave, Jeter, the captain and shortstop, walked in. "What time is it?" Rivera asked him.

"Seven after," Jeter said.

"You were supposed to be here seven minutes ago," Rivera said.

Posada, the catcher, was indeed the last to arrive. "Look at this," Rivera said, bowing his head at the table and rubbing the top of his balding pate. "See this? This is from Sado. He did this."

The Core Four were just getting warmed up. What follows is a transcript, edited for length and clarity, of their rare conversation: a celebration of their careers, their successes, their memories, their fears, but mostly their friendship.

SI: I want to go back to 1992, when Andy was throwing to Jorge, a converted second baseman, in Class A in Greensboro, N.C.

Posada: Go back to 1991. I was catching a bullpen from him [at short-season Class A] Oneonta, and he's throwing me knuckleballs. The ball hit me right in the knee. I said, "No more knuckleballs."

Pettitte: I had a knuckleball when I signed.

Jeter: Yeah, you're still throwing knuckleballs.

Pettitte: I'd get two strikes on somebody and throw it as hard as I could. Struck everybody out. And then they told me after the first year, "You've got to can it." They said, "After you've pitched for 10 years in the big leagues, if you want to break it back out, you can."

SI: So now you can throw it again.

Pettitte: It's no good now. I lost it.

SI: How about when Jeter showed up in Greensboro? He joined you guys on August 20, 1992.

Posada: [Laughs.] Good-looking fellow.

Rivera: Where was I?

SI: Fort Lauderdale, High A.

Posada: You were older. Let's make sure everybody knows that. He's the oldest.

Rivera: I saw Jeet…. Oh, my God. I was with my cousin [former major league outfielder Ruben Rivera] in Tampa. We were playing, if I'm not mistaken, the Cardinals in St. Pete. I looked at Jeet [who was in the Gulf Coast League before Greensboro]…. I was skinny? This boy was dying. I was like, Who is that?

Posada: He comes in the clubhouse, and he's got high tops, with an ankle brace. And

The Core Four—Rivera is 40; Posada, 38; Pettitte, 37; and Jeter, 35—have combined for 27 All-Star selections, 11 division titles, seven American League pennants, five world championships, and $562 million in career earnings.

remember that Louisville Slugger bag that you stick your bats in? He had that. I was like, Wow, this is our first-rounder?

Rivera: And throwing the ball away.… But I saw the hitting. He hit the ball hard, and far. I said, "Wow."

Posada: They changed the Peter Pan Section [in Greensboro]. It used to be behind first base. They had to move it to third base.

SI: That was where the kids sat?

Posada: Yeah, it was too dangerous [because of Jeter's throws].

Jeter: The stories get better and better every year.

SI: Mariano, I remember you once said you cried a lot in the minor leagues, right?

Rivera: Not that I cried a lot. I did cry, like two, three times. That was my second year, in Greensboro, 1991. Because I couldn't communicate. But imagine, I came from Panama. My first year, in Tampa, most of the people I played with spoke Spanish. So I was fine. My second year I went to Greensboro. And no Spanish at all. It was hard. I think that was one of the toughest times that I had.

SI: I think people would be surprised how tough it can be starting out for young players. You guys probably all had moments of doubt or thoughts of, Wow, I don't know if I can make it.

Jeter: I cried all the time—1992, when I first signed, similar to Mo. I had no roommate, because I signed late. Third baseman spoke no English. Second baseman spoke no English. I struggled for the first time. [Jeter hit .210 in his first season as a pro.] I cried almost every day. That was tough.

Posada: I went to junior college [in Decatur, Ala]. So I cried there. When I got to the pros it was, "This is what I want." It was exciting for me. But junior college was tough. I didn't know any English. I mean, I got to know it a lot better during junior college.

Pettitte: I didn't cry at all. But the toughest part for me was…I got called up to Oneonta

[in 1991, during his first season in the minors], and it's where all the older guys and the prospects were. Those were the guys from the four-year colleges, mostly. I'll never forget, they moved me up and I had nowhere to stay. They told me to get in touch with [former Yankees farmhand] Lyle Mouton and a couple of other guys living together in a house. It was like a two-bedroom home. They put a cot in the pantry of the kitchen for me, and I bought a little thing to hang my clothes on, like a hanging rack. That's where I stayed for the last month and a half that I was there. So that was a real tough time. I felt real uncomfortable because those guys were older than me.

SI: What about when you got to the big leagues? You all got there in 1995. Derek and Jorge, did you room together?

Posada: Well, they put us in the same hotel in New Jersey. We shared a car, to go back and forth to the ballpark. A Dodge Neon. It said NEON on the steering wheel, and if you [barely] touched it, touched the "O" just like this, it would honk the horn. Eh-eh. Just touch it. So Derek and I would be back and forth in the Neon. But in '95 we were watching most of the games. We didn't have a chance to play.

Jeter: That was in September. Mo and I came up earlier in '95, and they sent us down the same day [in June].

Rivera: I gave up a home run against Edgar Martínez. They got mad at me and Jeet and sent us both down.

Jeter: He gave up a home run and they sent me down! We were miserable.

SI: What about 1996? You won the championship, but is there something else about that year that's particularly memorable?

Posada: I got sent down like 10 times. I was in the big leagues for 60-something days. [He actually made four round trips between the minors and majors.] Up and down. I was in that elevator the whole year.

DEREK JETER

SI: Did you guys all have that moment of, I belong here. I can do this.

Jeter: Probably Opening Day in '96.

Pettitte: Didn't you hit a home run on Opening Day?

Jeter: Yeah.

Rivera: We were in Cleveland. We were snowed out, and then rescheduled.

Pettitte: For me that's when it all started. I mean, when Derek came along there was so much talk about him. I can't remember a whole lot of stuff. Like '95, I can't really remember…I remember Mo coming up and making some starts and being in the rotation and stuff like that. But everything's kind of like a blank for me in '95. But then in '96 when Derek came up, there was so much anticipation about him being our shortstop and Opening Day and that home run. I can remember that like it was yesterday.

SI: So how does your friendship come about? Do you start hanging out together off the field?

Jeter: Just around each other [at the ballpark]. You see them more than you see your family.

Pettitte: These guys [Jeter and Posada] are together 24/7, it seems like. But the four of us…I don't think we hang out…. I don't think we've ever been to lunch, us four, one time.

Posada: I don't think so.

Pettitte: But we spend so much time at the ballpark together, just talking.

Posada: We get on each other, we make fun of each other, we laugh….

Pettitte: If something's going on in the room, we can look at each other…

Posada: …and know what's going on—without even saying anything. I can just look at Derek, and he knows exactly what I'm thinking about. Mo same thing, Andy same thing.

Rivera: We have been together so long, but the four of us together, just us, like having breakfast, being all together at the same time? No, I don't think ever.

Posada: Maybe dinner, but part of a big group.

SI: If I wanted to get, say, restaurant advice, which one of you guys should I go to?

Jeter: Where are we?

SI: It depends where we are?

Rivera: [Points to Jeter.]

Posada: See, Mo goes to Benihana every day. So he would tell you to go to Benihana wherever we are.

Rivera: Listen, I like to simplify things.

SI: Okay, what if I was a young kid on the team and I wanted financial advice. Which one of you guys should I talk to?

Posada: Mo.

Rivera: You know what my son says? That I still keep the first dollar I made. I understand that we do this in a period of time. We cannot do this forever. So whatever you make, you have to make sure that you take care of it. At least that's what I do. I know I'm going to play this game for…a period of time.

Posada: Yeah, how long are you going to play, Mo?

Rivera: I have this year. After this year I don't have a contract. I don't have a job. I'm going to do whatever it takes to save the money that I have made, because I know that I'm not going to be working after that, or making the kind of money that we are making now. So you have to watch what you do, where you invest, and always make sure you do the right thing, and ask God definitely for directions.

SI: That was a good question, Jorge.

Pettitte: What was the question?

SI: How long are you going to do this? I'm assuming you guys all are in the same boat as far as that goes. Does anybody plan out, "I want to play X number of years?"

Rivera: I don't think so. I mean, how many times have I retired?

Jeter: He retires every other year.

Rivera: Every contract I think, Well, this is it for me.

Jeter: [Points at Pettitte.] Him, too. "This is my last year. One more year."

The heart of the Yankees' dynasty:
Jeter, Posada, Rivera, and Pettitte.

Pettitte: What are you talking about? I was [retired]. I was.

Rivera: I was retired every year after my contract was up. [But] I'm still going.

SI: This game keeps pulling you back.

Rivera: I love this game. This is what I know how to do. For me, it's kind of hard to just leave and be competitive. I'm competitive.

Jeter: It's tough to leave when you're having fun.

SI: You guys look like you still have fun after all these years, all these games, all these road trips. Am I right?

Jeter: You have to have fun. If I wasn't having fun, I couldn't play.

Pettitte: Especially after all the success we've had, right?

Rivera: I think it's easier for [Jeter] because he doesn't have a family. He can do this until… he'll be 40 and have no kids still. But to me, and I can talk about Andy and also Sado, you miss your kids. You miss your family. This year it has hit me hard, especially in spring training. My kids were in New York. I was in Tampa. And I was missing them a lot. So that line, where's your family and where's your game…how do you draw that line? How long are you going to do this? How long are they going to support you? And then flying, and those things that petrify you. I'm petrified by flights. I suffer on those flights.

SI: You guys must have fun with him about that.

Rivera: Are you kidding me? Everybody.

Joe Torre (left) and the Core Four during the ceremony
to retire Bernie Williams' number in 2015.

Posada: Every time the plane goes up and down we go, "Mo! Are you okay?"

Rivera: I loved it when we had [relief pitcher] Tom Gordon on the team. Because he would literally grab my hand. We'd be holding hands. He would say, "Mo, grab my hand!" He was maybe [more scared] than me…. You go through all those lines, but there is a line [where you can't play anymore]. And that's why I say [Jeter] is in a better position than us, to continue playing the game. I don't know how long I'm going to do this.

Pettitte: Because the older [your children] get, it gets harder. [Rivera's] oldest [16] is a year older than my oldest. More complications. It's pretty easy when they're small.

Posada: You've got kids who are driving now, right?

Pettitte: Not yet. Mo does. [His son] got his permit, so I guess he is driving.

Posada: So he's got the Challenger driving around? [Rivera owns a custom-built 2009 Dodge Challenger SRT8.]

Rivera: He wishes. But it's amazing. I remember my kid being this small, and now all of a sudden…. That's why I say it's hard. That's why I say there's a line and you have to know when to stop, even knowing that you love the game. To me my family is more important than the game.

SI: So tell me one thing about you guys that might be surprising. Like Derek, I know, is a practical joker.

Jeter: Me?

SI: He once tried to pull that trick on me about getting me to try to swallow a spoonful of cinnamon.

Posada: Well, he does that cinnamon thing, but that will be it for the whole year. He tries to see how many people he can get. And he will talk to every security guard, every new reporter. Derek's quiet, you know. He gets quiet.

Rivera: He's an instigator! Instigator!

Posada: The biggest instigator is over there—that lefty guy.

Pettitte: Actually, they all are!

Rivera: Whoa, timeout. Timeout. These three? Me? I'm in my corner. They all say, "Mo, this guy is talking about you!" Who do I instigate? Nobody. I'm on my own. This guy [Jeter]? The worst.

Pettitte: I'd say, to be fair, me, Jorgie, and Jeter, we stir it up pretty good.

Jeter: Yeah, we keep the clubhouse loose.

Posada: Mo, he's in charge of the relievers.

Pettitte: Mo's kind of the quiet assassin type. It goes on all the time. [Other players say] "Get Jeter off me." "Get Mo off me." I can't tell you how many times somebody has walked up to me and said, "What are you saying about me?"

Rivera: The beauty about this group of guys is it's family. As a family we all pull for one another. It's beautiful. I don't think you will have this, or see this, again—in any other sport. Period.

Posada: I have never been mad at any of these guys. I swear to God. Mad like we don't talk to each other? Never. If we have a problem, we talk about it and that's it. I don't think there's ever been any problem. I think we understand each other so well that we've never had a problem.

Jeter: What it comes down to is that I never have to worry about these guys being ready to play.

Pettitte: It's all about trust.

Jeter: I mean, it never crosses my mind. I don't have to worry about them. I know they know how to win. I know that's the only thing they care about. They don't care about their personal stats.

Rivera: No egos. No jealousy.

SI: It seems like you've always been that way.

Jeter: We learned that coming up. The Boss [George Steinbrenner], all he cared about was winning.

Rivera: Whatever they did, I think they brainwashed us! They did a good job, put it that way.

Posada: They taught us well. The coaches, the front office, the director of player development… they taught us well.

Rivera: You won't see this again. In any sport. Take a picture. And keep it.

SI: It seems like you guys always know you can count on one another.

Pettitte: Nothing against anybody else, but there are things I'll talk to these guys about that I may feel it's not appropriate to talk to somebody else about. There are certain things that may not need to be out there in the clubhouse. There's some stuff you feel like needs to be said between the four of us, and we'll say, "Hey, keep an eye on it."

Posada: Little things. We'll talk to each other and say, "What do you think about this?" And then we…

Jeter:…we've got to talk about it and make sure it doesn't happen again, things like that.

Posada: I bet you if we put our families together, they're very similar. I think my mom and dad are very similar to their moms and dads. Very, very similar.

Pettitte: No doubt. Very close.

Rivera: Strong families.

Posada: So I think that's why we're sitting here today.

SI: Thanks for your time, guys.

Jeter: Mo's going to Benihana's now. ●

Focusing on another at-bat
in Baltimore in 2011.

The Yankee captain cracks a smile
in Baltimore in 2011.

A fist bump for Mark Teixeira
in Boston in 2011.

Excerpted from SPORTS ILLUSTRATED, July 18, 2011

3,000 Reasons to Party

We choose the things we celebrate in sports and in life. Birthdays. Anniversaries. Weddings. Retirements. Why celebrate 3,000 hits? Why not? We all want a moment to celebrate

BY JOE POSNANSKI

Of course, Derek Jeter did not really get his 3,000th big league hit last Saturday under a clear blue sky at Yankee Stadium. No. He actually got his 3,184th hit…then 3,185…then 3,186…then 3,187…then 3,188. That would be if you count his postseason hits. But we don't count those. Why not? Well, why don't we celebrate a player for, say, reaching base 4,000 times? (Jeter passed 4,000 times on base last year.)

Why don't we celebrate 500 doubles or 2,000 RBIs or 4,000 innings pitched? Why don't we celebrate the Directors Guild Awards instead of the Oscars?

We choose the things we want to celebrate in sports and in life. We choose 3,000 regular-season hits as something to treasure. That was why Yankee Stadium on Saturday felt charged with excitement and nervousness and the buzz of anticipation. You don't need an irreproachable reason for a celebration. You need only a consensus.

Saturday was a good day to celebrate Derek Jeter for being one of the most splendid players in the game's history. It was a day game—baseball always seems a little bit better when it's played during the day. It was in New York, which is a great place to throw a party. A waft of a cool breeze blew. The game was sold out. Derek Jeter was nervous. He would not admit that part until later—"I've been lying to you guys for a long time," he would say after the game—but the nervousness wasn't hard to pick up. No Yankees player had ever reached 3,000 hits. Jeter visibly felt the burden of Yankees history.

Jeter led off for the 790th time in his career and engaged Tampa Bay starter David Price in an interesting little eight-pitch tango. Price threw eight fastballs, each from 92 to 95 mph.

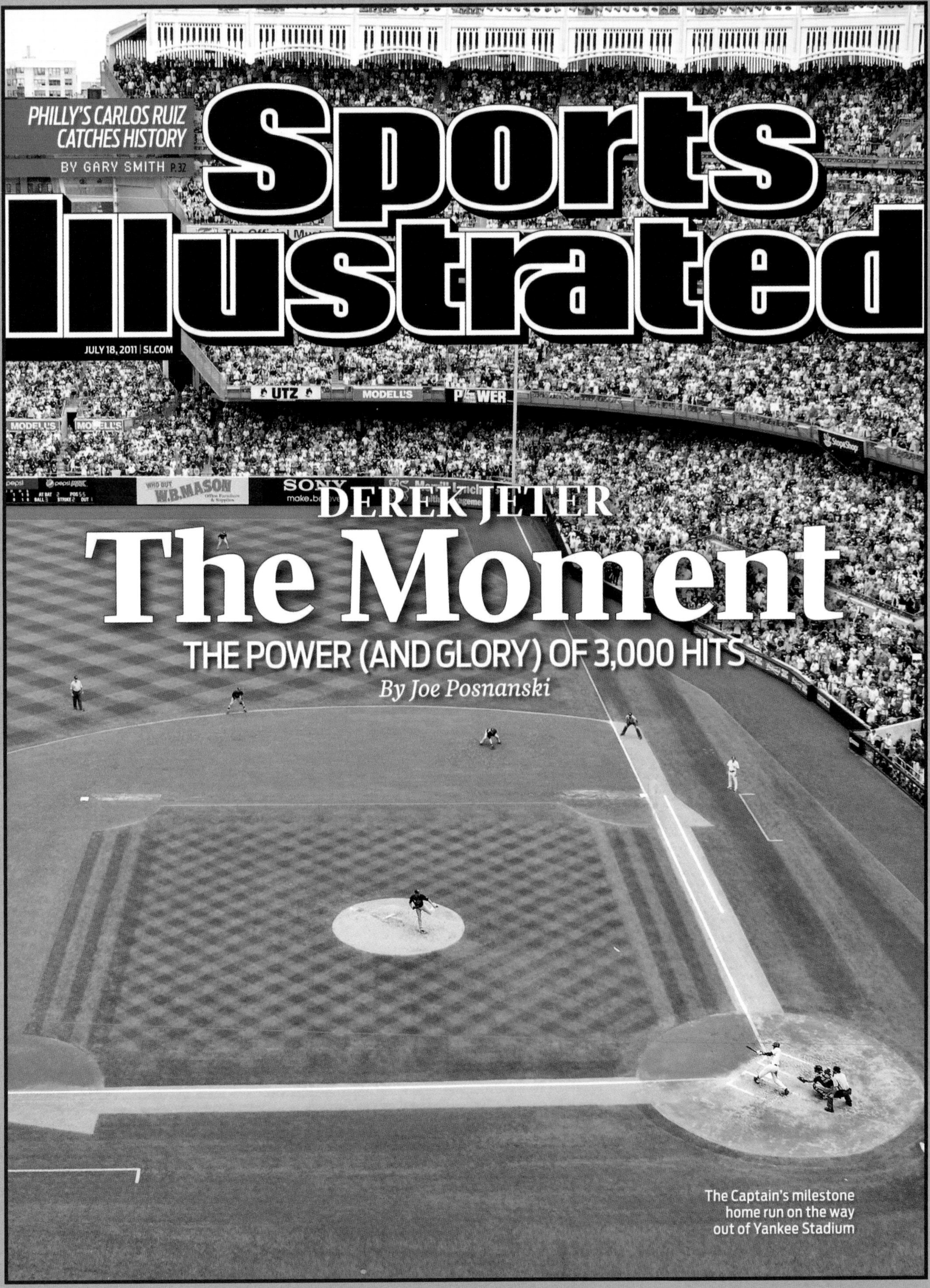

PHILLY'S CARLOS RUIZ
CATCHES HISTORY
BY GARY SMITH P.32

Sports Illustrated

JULY 18, 2011 | SI.COM

DEREK JETER

The Moment

THE POWER (AND GLORY) OF 3,000 HITS

By Joe Posnanski

The Captain's milestone
home run on the way
out of Yankee Stadium

On the sixth and seventh pitches Jeter fouled the ball into the stands, way late on both, though the crowd roared with expectation even on those. It is something to be in a full stadium where everyone in the place is rooting for the same thing. Finally, on that eighth fastball, Jeter chopped a ground ball that bounced between the Rays' shortstop and third baseman for a single. That was hit 2,999.

Jeter smiled as he stood at first base, as the loud cheers roared around him. "It was huge," he would say. He had worried—seriously worried—that he would not get the two hits he needed last weekend at Yankee Stadium. He was worried about a lot of stuff. He told everybody that he wasn't nervous. As he said: he was lying.

Derek Jeter got his actual 3,000th big league hit—counting postseason hits—in June of last year against Houston's Wandy Rodriguez. It was a home run. He hit another home run that day. And those were the last over-the-fence home runs he hit at Yankee Stadium for more than a year. This has been the most jolting part of watching Jeter the last year or so—the ball has stopped jumping off his bat. It thuds. Since that June day against Houston, he had slugged .323. That's slugging percentage. The young Derek Jeter had six seasons where his *batting average* was better than .323.

So, there was a vision of how he would get that 3,000th hit. A bloop over the second baseman was one possibility. A ground ball with eyes was another. "I just wanted to hit the ball hard," he would say. He stepped up to the plate against Price in the third inning, and the stadium filled with those loud cheers that people make when they are really cheering for themselves and a moment to remember.

Jeter stepped in. He touched his helmet. He held up his right hand to the umpire. He dug his cleats into the dirt. He arched his back. How many times have we seen this routine? How familiar has it become to fans who love Jeter and fans who despise Jeter and…well, those two

options more or less cover everybody. This time Price decided to show his repertoire. He got a called strike with a changeup, and Jeter fouled off another change. Jeter fouled off a fastball into the stands on the first-base side, at least 50 feet foul, but still people cheered with hope. It was, as Vin Scully likes to say, as if they were seeing the game with their hearts.

At exactly 2 p.m., with Jeter expecting fast-ball, with the crowd in high pitch, Price threw a 78-mph curveball that hung over home plate the way the sun hangs over Key West. And Jeter did the last thing anybody expected—including himself. He turned on it. He crushed it. As Jeter broke out of the box, he did not know if it would clear the fence. But he did know that nobody was going to catch it.

The ball went over the fence.

And then…madness. The Yankees' players rushed out of the dugout. The Rays' infielders clapped slightly. A 23-year-old man named Christian Lopez, who was given his ticket by his girlfriend, fell on the ball in the leftfield bleach-ers. The sound in the new stadium was as loud as it was in the old stadium when Jeter hit the home run in the 2001 World Series just after the clock struck midnight on Nov. 1. Jeter rounded the bases, and when he touched home plate, he ran into a bear hug from Jorge Posada. Incredible. Ridiculous.

There were details to sort out at that point. Jeter had become the second man to get his 3,000th hit on a homer; the other was Wade Boggs, who was famous much of his career for not hitting homers. Jeter became the 14th man to get his first 3,000 hits for one team, and the first to do it for the Yankees. And so on.

There were plenty of "and so ons" after that. The next time up, Jeter ripped a double to left. And so on. The time after that, he used an inside-out swing to punch a line drive to right-field, the sort of line drive Jeter has hit so often that it should be named for him. And so on. In the eighth inning, with the go-ahead run on

Jeter homers against the Rays for career hit number 3,000, the second player in history to hit a home run to reach that milestone (Wade Boggs was the first, in 1999).

third and the Rays' infield drawn in, Jeter hit a ground ball single, his fifth hit of the day. It was the second 5-for-5 game of his career, the first in more than a decade.

And so on…. Mariano Rivera closed the door with a perfect ninth inning, which Jeter would tell you is the way he would have dreamed for his 3,000-hit game to end. The crowd stayed for a long time to scream. Jeter stayed around to acknowledge them. Sinatra sang "New York, New York." Christian Lopez, the fan who caught the historic ball, gave it to Jeter for free because, he said, "it's his accomplishment." "Movie-ready," Yankees manager Joe Girardi would call it. And, yes, at some point it did feel like Robert Redford might just show up to throw a baseball with his son.

But perhaps the most striking part of all was how happy Derek Jeter was to have it over. He has worked hard through the years to keep many of his feelings private. He has worked hard

through the years to say the right things, to do the right things, to exemplify grace and class and confidence and humility, all at the same time. He is a proud athlete, and he has been growing old in front of America, and that cannot be easy.

On Saturday he played young again. He ripped the ball again. He got his 3,000th hit on a home run. His 3,003rd scored the winning run. And when the game ended, he talked mostly about relief. It's over, he said. We can move on now, he said. We will move on, of course. The All-Star Game was this week. The NFL lockout might come to an end. Rory McIlroy goes to the British Open. Jeter goes back to his battle with the years. It all moves very quickly. Saturday was a nice afternoon to stop for a moment. Why celebrate 3,000 hits? Hey, why not? •

The Yankees envelop
their captain at home plate
after hit number 3,000.

At Yankee Stadium,
hosting the Rays in 2011.

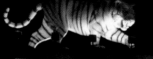

At bat against Justin Verlander in Detroit during the 2011 ALDS.

On deck against the Orioles
during the 2012 ALDS.

Jeter was never bothered by the bright lights of stardom.

A FOND FAREWELL

Jeter in the field against the Orioles in August of his final season.

Chapter 4

Excerpted from SPORTS ILLUSTRATED, February 24, 2014

Ride of the Yankee

Derek Jeter's career was a monument to excellence—and little else. Who will baseball re-create in his image?

BY JACK DICKEY

We learned on Feb. 12 that Derek Jeter would make the 2014 season his last in baseball on account of a combination of injuries and general fatigue. The timing sounds right: the Yankees' shortstop is on a one-year contract and will turn 40 this June, in the midst of his 20th campaign in the majors.

Jeter's exit shall no doubt fuel Yankees fans' existential dilemmas. Since 2010 they have watched the retirements of Andy Pettitte, Jorge Posada, Pettitte again, and Mariano Rivera. With Jeter, that cast made up the so-called Yankees' Core Four. But Jeter's departure looms larger than the others', for he has provided far more than routinely above-average contributions to a string of maddeningly successful baseball teams. What is Derek Jeter? He has represented singular team-centrism but also superstardom and celebrity. He has represented tireless effort but also effortless superiority. He has represented workaday reliability but also superhuman capacity in the most daunting circumstances. He has, it seems, come to stand for most anything. Jeter, with his five world championships and 3,000 hits, is big—but his myth is bigger.

The myth of Jeter owes everything to the circumstances of its creation. He could not have become Derek Jeter without playing in New York or for the Yankees. The city adores style and attitude—think of how New York fell for the pugnacious 1990s Knicks and Rex Ryan's semi-hapless Jets—but it has a soft spot for excellence, as anyplace else might. Jeter, granted a healthy head start of credibility by the pinstripes he wore and the triumphant but dusty history they evoke, quickly went about making excellence his signature trait.

He molded his Yankees in that image, compelling mid-to-late '90s New Yorkers to forget about George Steinbrenner's once meddlesome hand, transforming the Boss from baseball pariah into something of an elder statesman. Jeter's remaking of the team allowed Yankees fans to reject Alex Rodriguez (who won two MVP awards and a World Series in New York) as something less than a true Yankee.

Jeter announced in February the 2014 season would be his last.

The captain would
be leaving behind an
unparalled legacy.

It helped that the people ascendant in New York during the Age of Jeter—the people who would later fill, or not fill, the Legends Suites at the new Yankee Stadium—were themselves embracing success as style. Jeter, corporate in his on- and off-field comportment, rose in tandem with a buttoned-up and image-conscious Wall Street. When the team in 2002 launched the YES Network in partnership with Goldman Sachs, the pairing could hardly have been more fitting.

The Jeter myth, though, had to be spun and sent off to the masses somehow—no easy task, since the most famous ballplayer of his generation happened to be one of its least voluble. New York helped here too. The nation's media capital happens to house lots of daily newspapers (which mattered more then than now). To write about the team back then really meant to write about Jeter, the best player during a run of championships. Greater New York hardly contained a heart that the suave young ironman shortstop failed to capture.

Yet reportorial access has never guaranteed insight, and the relentlessly positive Jeter never gave away much about who he is. He worked hard, came from a good family, liked pretty women (Mariah Carey, Jessica Alba, Jessica Biel…). So Derek Jeter became the local writers' chimera, vivified by their gushing prose. He was a role model! He could do no wrong! He was the last man in baseball who would ever use steroids! (And you shut up about his glove!)

For all the good that Jeter's Boswells may have done him—their words seemed to echo in Jeter's advertisements for Nike, Gatorade, and Ford—they may too have done him a disservice. Their effusion led some naturally skeptical fans to question whether this guy from Kalamazoo, Mich., was all he was cracked up to be. A standout baseball player became a one-man referendum on media mythologizing.

Perhaps there's an even wider-reaching downside to the press' exuberant telling of the tale. After Jeter announced his plans to retire, a number of his successors in big-market stardom extolled his behavior. Mike Trout, David Wright, even Hanley Ramírez—they all spoke of how they'd modeled their careers, on and off the field, after Jeter's. Seriousness with their craft, blandness with the press—not a bad game plan, given all the success Jeter had with that approach.

But to what end? By now the rest of the media world has its attention fixed firmly on bigger men playing louder sports. Baseball, meanwhile, struggles in its search for a crossover star to inherit Jeter's mantle. That's not his problem. He never asked to be Derek Jeter.

In a surprise, the usually social-media-shy Jeter didn't leave the news of his retirement to his myth-makers. He announced his exit with a 703-word Facebook post in which he wrote of wanting to embark on new challenges in philanthropy and business. One such business, unveiled in November, is Jeter Publishing, an imprint of Simon & Schuster. He says he'll be closely involved. Somehow, Derek Jeter's definition by way of the written word is just beginning. •

During a July home game
against the Rays in 2014.

Even toward the end of his final season, Jeter drove himself for every extra base.

With the Yankees out of the playoffs, Jeter was left to ponder his future beyond the game.

Staring across the field at the visiting Royals during one of his last homestands at Yankee Stadium.

Excerpted from SI.com, September 7, 2014

Saying Goodbye to a Legend

As his legendary career comes to a close, Derek Jeter was center stage for a farewell ceremony at Yankee Stadium

BY JAY JAFFE

The Yankees' 2014 season is dwindling in its opportunities to do everything, it seems, except to celebrate Derek Jeter. Barring some as-yet-unforeseen tear with an underachieving lineup and a makeshift rotation, the Yankees will finish outside the playoff picture for the second straight season, the first time that has happened since 1992–93, which is to say the years 4 and 3 B.D.J. Before… well, you get it.

It should have been awkward to celebrate even a Hall of Fame-bound player under such circumstances, particularly one who hardly relishes the attention paid to his individual accomplishments ahead of those of his team. But on Sunday in the Bronx, the Yankees bulldozed such awkwardness by doing what they do best: over-the-top pomp. They swung for the fences in Ruthian—or more aptly, Steinbrennerian—fashion, providing a respite from the present reality surrounding the team and the day's honoree via a star-spangled gala. While they didn't get the usually stoic Jeter to summon the waterworks, the 40-year-old team captain made clear that he enjoyed the stops they pulled out.

"It was awesome," he said following the game, a 2–0 loss to the Royals. "The Yankees know how to throw big ceremonies. To be part of it, having all those people come out there to honor you and show their support, and the fans, the way they treated me, this is something that I'll remember forever.

"I enjoyed every minute of it. But when I was done speaking and people were standing around, I thought it was time to say, 'We've got to play a game.'"

The captain acknowledges the crowd during Derek Jeter Day at Yankee Stadium on Sept. 7, 2014.

That the focus would fall on Jeter under such circumstances—fading playoff hopes, another lifeless showing from their offense—was inevitable, though hardly unprecedented. Just a year ago, Mariano Rivera played the same Farewell Circuit as the Yankees missed the playoffs for the first time since 2008 and the second time since 1993. The difference there—apart from Rivera's preternatural grace and sincere desire to connect with fans, players, and ballpark employees as he took his last lap around the majors—was that the great closer, if not at the absolute zenith of his career, was still good enough to rank among the game's best. Nobody would have batted an eye had he put a halt to the festivities and instead chose to continue pitching his 60 innings a year, even at age 44.

Jeter, on the other hand, is limping toward the finish line, in the throes of a dreadful post-July slump that makes for awkward questions and suggestions. Should he volunteer to hit lower in the order? Should manager Joe Girardi nail him to the bench and play the even lighter-hitting Stephen Drew or Brendan Ryan at short? Coming into Sunday's game hitting .260/.306/.311, he's no longer good enough to merit everyday play except on reputation, and hasn't been since that October 2012 night when his left ankle gave way as he chased a ground ball.

Sure, you can scroll through the ranks of everyday shortstops and imagine that plugging in a better one—or a younger, healthier model of the Captain—to replace this replacement-level shell would place the Yankees in a playoff-bound position. But given a lineup with perhaps two regulars (Jacoby Ellsbury and Brett Gardner) meeting or exceeding expectations, and a rotation missing three-fifths of its preseason blueprint, an upgrade at shortstop would have made little difference in the grand scheme.

Hardly the best atmosphere to throw a party, perhaps, but as with the way a playoff-free team closed out The House That Ruth Built back in 2008, the Yankees went ahead and did so in gaudy fashion. They plastered the Jeter Final Season Logo (capitalized, ahem) everywhere: on patches for their pinstriped uniforms, on a ring of flags flying around the top of Yankee Stadium, on the grass in foul territory down the first- and third-base lines, and on the baseballs used for Sunday's game. In the Great Hall, the stadium's outer concourse, they unveiled a 30-foot-by-30-foot photo banner of Jeter connecting for one of his 3,449 hits, larger than life for all to see.

The Yankees brought in his family: grandmother Dorothy Connors ("The reason why I was a Yankees fan," Jeter said later), parents Dr. Charles and Dot, sister Sharlee, and nephew Jalen. Dozens of "Jeter's Leaders" from

"I enjoyed every minute of it. But when I was done speaking and people were standing around, I thought it was time to say, 'We've got to play a game.'"

his Turn 2 Foundation took the field for the ceremony as well. Also on hand for the festivities were several former teammates from championship teams: David Cone, Tino Martinez, Hideki Matsui, Paul O'Neill, Jorge Posada, Tim Raines, Rivera, Bernie Williams, and Gerald Williams, plus former head athletic trainer Gene Monahan. From among the "Core Four," only Andy Pettitte was missing due to the oldest excuse in the book, an elk-hunting commitment with his son. Commissioner-elect Rob Manfred showed up, as did Reggie Jackson, "Mr. October" to Jeter's "Mr. November," and for some reason, MLB Network broadcaster Harold Reynolds.

Former manager and recent Cooperstown inductee Joe Torre was also on hand, and prior to the game shared a favorite memory from 1996, the first full major league season of the shortstop's career:

"The first year, the first playoff game we had against Texas, I think he made an error that could have contributed to losing a game. I was asked by one of the media if I felt I had to talk to him, the fact that he was a rookie, devastation and all that stuff. I said, 'I'll figure that out. If I need to, I will.'

"On his way out of the clubhouse, he peeks into my office—he was on his way home—and says, 'Mr. Torre, get your rest tonight. Tomorrow is the most important game of your life.'

"I said, 'I don't need to talk to him.'"

Prior to the festivities, Girardi expressed concern that with a game to follow, Jeter might not fully immerse himself in the occasion: "I hope he has the chance to take in the magnitude of the moment. But that's not his personality." But Jeter, unaware of exactly what the Yankees had planned for him, did manage to do so, at least to a point. "I didn't go in with any expectations. I was surprised by a few of the people that showed up."

Indeed, among the surprise guests introduced later in the festivities were a trio of Hall of Famers: Dave Winfield, Jeter's idol growing up; Cal Ripken Jr., the player who provided the template for a generation of tall, offense-minded shortstops; and Michael Jordan, the superstar who provided the template for athlete-as-multinational brand. The Yankees reached even further into the stratosphere for other special guests: a trio of astronauts on the International Space Station replicated the "Re2pect" salute while floating in zero gravity.

Following the special guests, various Steinbrenners and Yankees officials came bearing gifts: a massage therapy machine, a frame with patches from Jeter's 14 All-Star appearances, a 10-day trip to Tuscany, a check for $222,222.22 to Jeter's Turn 2 Foundation, a Waterford crystal bearing an inscription (again?), even a proclamation from New York City mayor Bill de Blasio declaring Sept. 7, 2014, as "Derek Jeter Day." All that was missing was a funeral pyre on the mound to send Jeter into the afterlife.

For as over the top as it was, and for as much Jeter Fatigue as the average fan has by now (particularly after this year's All-Star Game turned into its own Jeter lovefest), none of it would have happened without the player's singular résumé— 14 All-Star appearances, five World Series rings, the No. 6 spot on the all-time hits list, and the top spot on that and several other Yankees leaderboards—or the near-universal respect of those with and against whom he's played. You can roll your eyes at the media characterizations of the values that Jeter embodies, and the frequency with which words like "special" and "class" pop up when teammates and opponents describe him, but his peers aren't merely paying lip service when they speak of his focus, his tireless work ethic, or the positive example he has set during his career. They genuinely view him that way, and strive to emulate him, on and off the field. Hence stuff like this "One Word for 2" tribute page on MLB.com from other stars, specially assembled for the occasion.

The pregame ceremony wrapped up with a brief address from Jeter. After thanking the

Steinbrenner family, his own family and friends, and his managers, coaches, and teammates, here's what Jeter told the crowd of 48,110:

"Lastly, most importantly, I want to thank you, the fans. Everyone that's here today, anyone that's at home watching, anyone that's ever been here over the course or watched during the last 20 seasons, thank you very much.

"You guys have all watched me grow up over the last 20 years. I watched you too. Some of you guys getting old too. But I want to thank you for helping me feel like a kid for the last 20 years.

"In my opinion, I've had the greatest job in the world. I got a chance to be the shortstop for the New York Yankees, and there's only one of those. And I always felt as though that my job was to try to provide joy and entertainment for you guys, but it can't compare to what you brought me. So, for that, thank you very much."

Of course there was still the small matter of a game to play, one of the more unusual aspects of the festivities. As Jeter described it afterwards:

"We have three weeks left in the season and we're trying to win games, so it was a unique situation. I don't know if there's many people who've been in that situation, so it's kind of tough to explain how you feel. You appreciate all the support, the kind words that people are saying, but at the same time, I'm still trying to play a game. It's difficult to juggle at times."

In a scene that recalled what the American League All-Stars did for Rivera at Citi Field last summer—staying back in the dugout while the closer took the mound and the spotlight alone—Jeter's teammates remained behind as he ran onto the field prior to the national anthem and received yet another ovation. "I do the same thing every game, so I was unaware of the fact that no one was behind me," he said later, allowing a bit of his deadpan wit to peek through. "Chase [Headley] and [Martín] Prado are usually next to me during the anthem, and when I saw they weren't there, I turned around

and saw no one was out there. First thought is that I messed up and ran out there too early."

Even during the game, the tributes continued. The Yankees slapped adulatory quotations alongside each player's visage on the centerfield DiamondVision as he came to bat ("I've always admired Derek from afar, and getting a chance to play with him this season has been an experience that I'll never forget"—Brian McCann), and play videotaped congratulations from the varied likes of Robinson Canó (who drew boos from a large segment of the crowd), Billy Crystal, Eli Manning, Regis Philbin, Seth Rogen, and Buck Showalter.

Alas, Jeter couldn't produce the kind of fireworks that made July 9, 2011—the day his home run off David Price kicked off a 5-for-5 performance that carried him over the 3,000 hit threshold—just one of the signature events of his career. But he did get on base twice in his four plate appearances, no small accomplishment for a player who came in hitting .209/.230/.264 since the start of August, getting on base multiple times in just six out of 31 games.

In the first inning against Royals starter Yordano Ventura, Jeter collected an infield single on a grounder hit into the 5.5 hole, one that could only have been prevented by the kind of Jeter jump throw that he used to pull off a decade and a half ago; not even the rangy Alcides Escobar was up to the task, for his long, arced toss arrived late. Later, he worked a six-pitch walk in the third inning, though Ventura struck him out in the fifth.

Unfortunately, as has so often been the case this season, the rest of The Offense Formerly Known as the Bronx Bombers wasn't up to the task of providing support. Lacking Gardner—improbably, their leader in slugging percentage (.442) and OPS+ (121)—due to an abdominal injury, they couldn't even score two for 2. They collected just two additional singles and three walks during Ventura's six-plus

innings, and advanced a runner to second base just twice; forget about third or home.

Meanwhile, Yankees starter Shane Greene labored through a 29-pitch first inning without giving up a run, but he wasn't so lucky in the second inning, as a Josh Willingham swinging bunt single, a Mike Moustakas single, and his own throwing error on a Norichika Aoki grounder produced a run. The Royals took advantage of another error in the third inning, when Carlos Beltran dropped Alex Gordon's flyball; Gordon stole second and came home on Eric Hosmer's single, though Hosmer was thrown out 9-2-6-4 trying to stretch it into a double.

Once Ventura departed, the Yankees fared little better against the Royals' lights-out bullpen of Aaron Crow, Kelvin Herrera, and Wade Davis, going 1-for-8 while grounding into a double play to erase the runner Ventura left behind to start the seventh. A Beltran single to lead off the ninth inning brought the tying run to the plate, but Davis sandwiched strikeouts of McCann and Drew around a Mark Teixiera groundout to preserve the victory.

With the loss, the Yankees fell to 73–68, 9½ behind the Orioles in the AL East race, and 4½ back in the Wild Card race with the Tigers (one back) and the Indians (3½ back) ahead of them. They began the day with their playoff odds at 2.9 percent, and they're now lower. The season and Jeter's career are one game closer to their inevitable conclusion. ●

Excerpted from SI.com, September 26, 2014

"Tomorrow" Arrives for Derek Jeter

In his final Yankee Stadium game, Derek Jeter fought back his emotions to deliver yet another iconic moment

BY TED KEITH

Tomorrow, he said. Ask me tomorrow.

That was Derek Jeter's repetitive response on Wednesday afternoon when reporters tried to get him to address what it would feel like when he played the final home game of his Hall of Fame career at Yankee Stadium against the Baltimore Orioles on Thursday. What would he think? How would he feel? How would it all end?

Tomorrow. Tomorrow. Tomorrow.

He would betray no emotion, allow for no sentimentality. For a player always criticized for his defense, the 40-year-old Jeter has always had a first-rate defense mechanism. It has at times made him seem aloof, if not unfeeling, and seemed to create a barrier between himself and the fans and media who desperately wanted to know the real him.

When tomorrow finally arrived, Jeter gave everyone, especially the sellout crowd of 48,613, a glimpse at the player they have come to love and revere and the man he almost never let them see. He smoked the night's biggest hit (of course), an opposite-field single (of course) in the bottom of the ninth that won the game for the Yankees, 6–5 (of course).

And then he came as close as he ever has to letting his guard down in public. His beaming smile and his exultant reaction as Antoan Richardson slid home with the winning run was straight out of a Giuliani Era-October night, but the next several minutes were something new. He warmly embraced his teammates and ex-teammates—which included the rest of the Core Four, Andy Pettitte, Jorge Posada, and Mariano Rivera—and his family on the field, took several curtain calls from the adoring fans, then walked out to shortstop, which he had just

Jeter takes the field for his
final game at Yankee Stadium.

played for the last time, and knelt down to say a prayer.

With the Yankee Stadium speakers blasting Frank Sinatra's "My Way," he rose, and, in an ending topped only by the one he had delivered with his bat moments before, doffed his cap and walked off the field for the last time, just as the final notes echoed throughout the ballpark.

Later, when he could finally be asked what "tomorrow" had been like, Jeter was perhaps more honest and open than he had been at any point in his 20 major league seasons. The first question, on the field, was about what he thought when he went to the plate for the last time: "Don't cry," he said.

Later, in the press conference, he said, "I don't know how I played tonight. These last few weeks have been very difficult. It's gotten more and more difficult as we got to today."

And: "I think I've done a pretty good job of controlling my emotions. I have them. I try to hide them."

And: "Sometimes I have to trick myself, convince myself, whether it's pain [or whatever], that I don't have it. Today I wasn't able to do it. I was almost thinking to myself, [Manager] Joe [Girardi], get me out of here before I do something to cost us this game."

And: "At times [the season] has been difficult because you feel like you're watching your own funeral."

And: "This was above and beyond everything I've ever dreamed of. I've had a dream since I was four or five years old, and part of that dream is over now."

And: "Look, I have emotions. I just think I have a pretty good poker face."

Not on this day. The game was only one inning old, but already the weight of the day was taking its toll on the evening's honored guest. He had almost broken down in his car that afternoon on his drive to the stadium. He had turned away to conceal his emotions before the game when his teammates presented him with a painting—the original version of the recent cover of *The New Yorker* that featured him—and a watch in the clubhouse. He forgot his elbow guard when he went to the on-deck circle in the bottom of the first. And he spent the early innings looking around the place that had been his home for the past six seasons, and, in a sense, for the last two decades, and fighting back tears.

He betrayed no emotion outwardly, especially not when he lashed an RBI double off the left-centerfield wall in his first at-bat. But when he returned to his position at shortstop in

> **"**
>
> **The first question, on the field, was about what he thought when he went to the plate for the last time: "Don't cry," he said.**

Jeter salutes the fans during his final game in New York.

the top of the second, so did his nerves. *Please don't hit the ball to me*, he thought as a new round of haunting "De-rek-Je-ter" chants filled the cool evening air. New York third baseman Chase Headley looked over and saw the always-stoic Yankees captain on the verge of being overcome.

"Hey," he said. "You can't leave."

It was meant as a nod to something Jeter often says in batting practice when a player hits a ball off the wall. Headley had hoped it would break his teammate's tension and elicit a laugh. Jeter could only smirk.

Jeter, of course, is leaving. After 1,391 games, 5,517 at-bats, and 1,727 hits, he played his last game at Yankee Stadium and made sure it was one neither he nor anyone else would ever forget. All night he was at the center of the action. There was his double in the first inning, a fine play ranging to his left—take note, haters—that started a replay-approved double play in the third, and a fielder's choice that, coupled with an error, plated two runs to give New York a 4–2 lead in the seventh.

The margin was 5–2 in the top of the ninth when Jeter jogged out to his position one last time. If a plan existed to remove him before the third out, none of the rest of the Yankees were aware of it. Closer David Robertson came in and, with one out, yielded a two-run homer to Baltimore's Adam Jones that trimmed the gap to 5–4. With two out, Steve Pearce launched another home run to tie the score.

Robertson avoided further damage and as the Yankees trudged off the field, their teammates in the dugout immediately noticed something else: Jeter was due up third in the bottom of the ninth.

"Everybody's finishing each other's sentences, saying, 'Here's what's going to happen,'" said backup infielder Brendan Ryan. "'[DH José] Pirela's going to get a hit, [Brett] Gardner's going to bunt him over, and Jeter's going to walk them off.'"

Pirela did indeed get a hit, lacing a single to left field. Richardson came in to pinch-run, and Gardner did indeed bunt him over. Jeter then lashed at the first pitch from reliever Evan Meek, ripping it into rightfield where Baltimore's Nick Markakis, blessed with one of the game's best arms, came up throwing.

"I think we would have had to charge the outfield if he threw him out," said Headley later.

He didn't. Richardson was safe, and the same players who had predicted what would happen then bolted out of the dugout to mob Jeter between first and second. It was a moment that immediately took its place among the most memorable of Jeter's career, on par with any of the Dives, Flips, and October—and November—heroics that have been the touchstones of his Hall of Fame résumé.

When Jeter's career officially comes to an end this weekend in Boston—he'll DH at least once, but offered no specifics on how many games he'd play—those are the moments that will echo far beyond his statistics and the overheated debate that always surrounded them.

"Luck gravitates toward certain people," Ryan said when asked how it could be that one player would always find himself in the middle of such situations. "There's a reason those moments find certain people. I don't think it's coincidental that it keeps happening for him."

It won't happen anymore, not for Jeter and maybe not for anyone else. No other player of his generation has provided so many signature moments, and it would be foolish to expect a player in future generations to have as many.

Despite what Headley told him, and despite the outpouring of love from the fans and the respect from his opponents—even the Orioles stayed in the dugout and applauded after he had just beaten them—Jeter is leaving. Not because he can't play anymore, he said Thursday night, but because he doesn't want to. There are only yesterdays now for Jeter in the Bronx. But the memories of them will fill an awful lot of tomorrows. •

Taking the field in the Bronx for one last time.

All eyes were on the captain during his final Yankee Stadium appearance.

Jeter scripted a Hollywood ending, hitting a walk-off single in his final Yankee Stadium at-bat.

Jeter celebrates his
game-winning single.

Excerpted from Sports Illustrated, September 29, 2014

Exit Stage Center

Derek Jeter might not be the most famous ballplayer ever, but he's certainly the most familiar. In a series of revealing interviews, the Yankees' shortstop reflects on how he survived being watched, photographed, praised, and poked like no one else, and what has changed in the game (lots) and in himself (little) over two decades in the New York glare

BY TOM VERDUCCI

In the rare moments when he reflects on his career, as on this September afternoon before his last game in Baltimore's Camden Yards, or when he has neither bat nor glove in hand, Derek Jeter absentmindedly pulls on the bill of his cap with two hands, thumbs on the underside, fingers atop. There it is again. Even the small idiosyncrasies of Jeter have become so well-known.

He is sitting in a golf cart outside the Yankees' clubhouse, fresh from his daily work in the batting cage. Only two weeks remain before the most familiar baseball player there ever was plays for the final time.

"The game has changed a lot," he says. "The way the game is played. Now it's more analytics and shifts and tendencies and pitch counts, and that really didn't exist when I first came up."

"Is that a change for the better?" I ask him.

"It's just change," he says, and then even he has to mock his diplomacy with a smile and a laugh. "It's a change, yeah."

"What about change off the field?"

"You have to assume that everything you do is public knowledge," he says. "Everything. Because now everyone is a reporter. Everyone is a photographer. Someone can take a picture and make a story, which has happened plenty of times, and twist it and turn it anyway they want to. You used to be able to go out...it's all I've known. I've been here since I was 20."

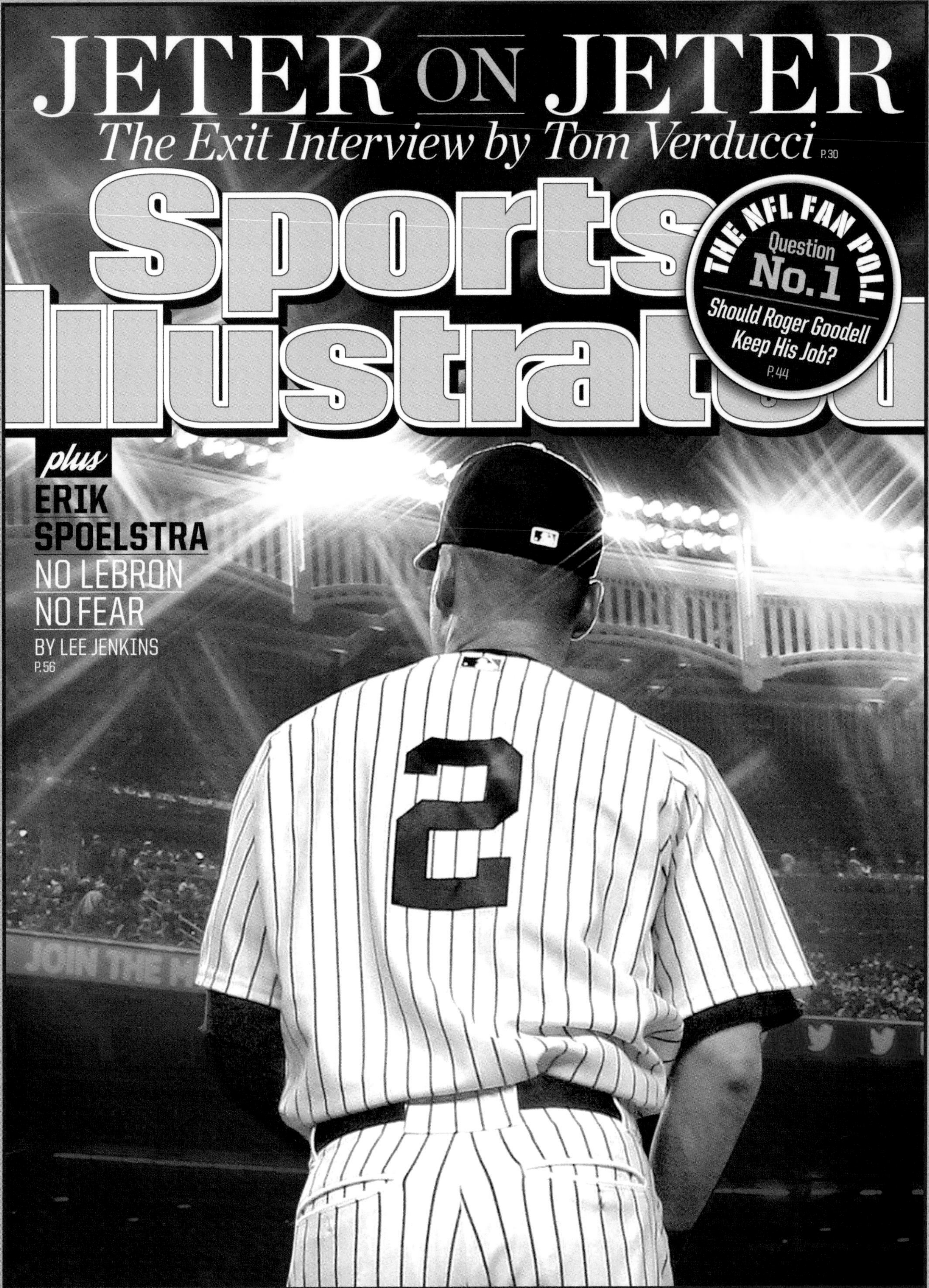

JETER ON JETER

The Exit Interview by Tom Verducci P.30

Sports Illustrated

THE NFL FAN POLL.
Question
No. 1
Should Roger Goodell
Keep His Job?
P.44

plus

ERIK SPOELSTRA

NO LEBRON NO FEAR

BY LEE JENKINS
P.56

JOIN THE M

He tugs on the brim of his cap.

Derek Jeter may not be as famous in the legendary sense as Babe Ruth or Willie Mays, but he is the most familiar player there ever was, because no other ballplayer spent more time in the public eye than Jeter. He is the most influential and popular player in the sport's greatest era of growth. It's not just that he has gotten the most hits and played the most games since the 1994–95 players' strike. It's also that he grew up as a champion New York Yankee, spending nearly every October on national television. With the help of an expanded postseason and the last foreseeable dynasty, Jeter played nearly an entire season's worth of playoff games—158, more than anybody in history. He played 71 times on *Sunday Night Baseball*, also more than any other player. He has hits in 42 different ballparks. His number 2 jersey has been the top-selling jersey in baseball in six of the past seven years, missing the mark only during his injury-shortened 2013 season.

No one has been covered more or played in front of more people—either live or on a screen of some kind. Hence the familiarity with all things Jeter. It's not just the Brim Tug. So much about him is famous enough to be recognizable by shorthand. The Maier Homer. The Flip. The Dive. Mr. November. The Jump Throw. The Jeterian Swing. The Homer for 3,000. The Five Rings. The Fist Pump. Captain Clutch. Number 2.

Many of those who would be Jeter fell hard around him. Five of the top 10 vote-getters for the 2002 All-Star Game (the last season before PED testing) would be tainted by connections to steroid use. Meanwhile, Jeter arrived in the nation's largest media market at the age of 20 and put in 20 seasons there. The only other baseball player to last 20 years in New York is Mel Ott, and he was finished with the Giants in 1947, before the World Series was broadcast on national television.

Jeter played his first game in 1995, two years after the Web browser was introduced; he won his first championship in '96, the year of the first high-definition broadcast; he was named to his first All-Star Game in '98, the year Google was founded; he was third in the American League MVP voting in '99, the year the commercial camera phone was introduced; he won the World Series MVP in 2000, as the Yankees began to form the YES Network; he notched his 2,000th hit in 2006, the first season with TMZ and Twitter.

Yet here he stands, through two decades in Gotham—during the ascent of an information age that devalues privacy and discretion—with integrity intact, hardly a scratch on him. The element most associated with Jeter is winning: over the past 100 years only Pete Rose, Hank Aaron, and Carl Yastrzemski played in more wins than Jeter's 1,722 regular-season and postseason victories, and combined they have fewer World Series rings. But a close second on Jeter's career marquee is the way he kept above the fray. "At times probably a lot of the media gets frustrated with me," he says. "But for me the only way I'm able to operate here for this long is I don't like negativity. I don't like to talk about it. I don't like to answer questions about it.

"I always hear people say I give the same answers or I don't give you much. No, I just don't give you much negativity. When people are negative a lot, it starts to creep into your mind, and then you start having doubts, and I don't like that. If there's another way, show me. My job is to stay positive. My job is to limit distractions. And if you get annoyed by that, I don't expect you to understand because you're not in my shoes."

The last days of Jeter's career have been a celebration of what he represents, especially with his .255 batting average for the worst Yankees team in 22 years providing few current highlights. Fans in Arlington, Texas, cheered wildly when a call was reversed against their Rangers in favor of Jeter's getting a hit. Fans in Kansas City gave him a standing ovation after his final at-bat there, a groundout. Baltimore fans ran down

> "
>
> So much about him is famous enough to be recognizable by shorthand. The Maier Homer. The Flip. The Dive. Mr. November. The Jump Throw. The Jeterian Swing. The Homer for 3,000. The Five Rings. The Fist Pump. Captain Clutch. Number 2.

aisles in droves to snap his picture as he stood in the on-deck circle. *FORTUNE* ranked him the 11th greatest leader in the world, 22 spots ahead of Apple CEO Tim Cook. Astronauts in the International Space Station tipped their caps to him in zero gravity. Gene Simmons of the rock group KISS called him "a very powerful and attractive man." A New Jersey farmer created a five-acre corn maze in the shape of his face. His game-used uniforms are selling for $25,000.

How could the most familiar of all players have held up this long and this well? I sat with him for a series of exclusive interviews in his last month as a player to search for explanations—to have Jeter explain Jeter.

The day Jeter reported to the Gulf Coast League Yankees in Tampa in 1992 he found himself standing over a bin filled with wood bats. Jeter, the Yankees' first-round draft choice and sixth overall, had used only a metal bat at Central High School in Kalamazoo, Mich. He picked through the wood bats until he found one that in size and shape most resembled what he'd swung in high school. It was a Louisville Slugger P72, a model first crafted in 1954 for a minor leaguer named Les Pinkham. This one was 34 inches long and weighed 32 ounces.

From that first day in pro ball to what will be his last, covering more than 15,000 turns at-bat, Jeter never used another model. "Maybe I'd pick up another one in batting practice if I broke one," he says. "But I've never had an at-bat in a game with another one."

Once you know that hitters often treat their bats the way middle schoolers do the objects of their affection, you understand how downright odd it is that Jeter never tried a different bat from age 18 to 40. "The thing I'll tell my grandkids about with Derek is how much I learned about the importance of routine," says Yankees catcher Brian McCann. "He is fanatical about preparation. He does the same thing every day: his work in the cage, his ground balls, his BP. He never deviates."

I ask Jeter who influenced this belief in routine.

"No one," he says. "You learn what's best for you. I've always been a believer in hard work and no excuses. I would never want to play a game and be unsuccessful and think, Well, I could have been successful if I had done this. You know how sometimes we don't have BP and they make it optional? It's usually optional because I want to hit."

If a praying mantis could swing a baseball bat, it would hit like Jeter. His swing is a series of bent limbs folding and unfolding around a torso bent at the waist that falls toward the plate. His left foot comes up and down twice. His hands dip the bat barrel back slightly before it comes forward. His left elbow flies out. The last guy to put up such great numbers with such an unorthodox swing was Arnold Palmer.

An influence: Gary Denbo. He was Jeter's first manager, during that summer of 1992. Denbo didn't try to change Jeter's swing. "He saw what I was and just tried to make it better," Jeter says. Except for five seasons when Denbo was with other organizations, Jeter has worked with him every off-season.

Another influence: Gerald Williams. The Yankees invited Jeter to his first major league spring training in his second season out of high school. The '93 Yankees were loaded with veterans who enjoyed picking on young players. Jeter didn't know any of them. Williams, 26 then, looked out for the 18-year-old Jeter like a big brother, always ready with counsel and encouragement.

The Yankees assigned Jeter that year to Greensboro, where he committed 56 errors, and then to the Instructional League in Tampa. Because of an injury to his left hand, Jeter was unable to hit in Tampa. It became a six-week defensive boot camp under another influence, coach Brian Butterfield. Butterfield changed the way Jeter threw (shortening his arm swing so that he didn't drop the ball below his waist) and the way he caught (showing him how to "take" the baseball rather than always catching it with "give").

"It was six weeks of only defense," Jeter says. "It turned my career around."

Jeter made his big league debut two years later, playing 15 games in 1995. The next season, when Joe Torre replaced Buck Showalter as Yankees manager, New York had its starting shortstop for the next 19 years. Jeter was assigned a locker in the same row as a 36-year-old out-fielder who came to the park every day with a smile, even though he was a seven-time All-Star

reduced to part-time work. Tim Raines, the one Yankee who could laugh off a slump or needle Paul O'Neill about beating up a watercooler, became another influence.

"I learned from him to have fun," Jeter says. "He had fun every day. That's a big part of being able to play all those years: to enjoy yourself."

The only time Jeter left a postseason game before the eighth inning was when the Yankees had a chance to win the 2001 World Series in Phoenix. Their Game 6 potential clincher deteriorated rapidly when the Diamondbacks hit Andy Pettitte like they knew what was coming. It turns out they did: Pettitte was tipping his pitches. The score was 4–0 when Torre replaced him in the third inning with a journeyman reliever named Jay Witasick. Eight of the next nine batters raked Witasick for hits. By the time Torre pulled Witasick, it was 13–0; the game was so hopeless that in the fifth Torre pulled Jeter, catcher Jorge Posada, and first baseman Tino Martinez. Jeter left the dugout for his locker to change from his metal spikes to turf shoes. Witasick, who had allowed eight earned runs, still the most in World Series history, sat in the training room. What Jeter heard from him there infuriated him.

"Well," the pitcher said, "at least I had fun."

"What!" Jeter shouted. Posada would later say that Jeter "jumped all over" the pitcher: "That was the angriest I've ever seen him."

Witasick had violated a core Jeter belief: he took losing too easily. I asked Jeter if it bothered him when teammates didn't want to win as badly as he did. "Of course," he says. "I think most people want to win at anything. But the thing that separates you is if losing bothers you."

I ask him if he can change a teammate in that regard.

"I don't think so," he says. "Either something means something to you or it doesn't. I don't think you can teach someone to have something mean something to them, do you know what I mean?"

Jeter grew up in a Yankees minor league system in which winning was more important than player development. For instance, the catering for Jeter's Rookie League team in Tampa—strip steak, meatloaf, corn dogs—depended on how well the team was playing. "Losing really bothered the Boss," Jeter says, referring to late Yankees owner George Steinbrenner. "It was stressed—preached to us—on every level of the minor league system that winning was the most important thing, which is why I always got along so well with the Boss. We had the same mind-set."

Truth is, Jeter was wired to win before he went to work for Steinbrenner. "I probably got it from my dad," he says. "He used to beat me at everything when I was younger. He never let me win. No, no, no, not at all. You've got to earn it. Things aren't given to you."

Today we are sitting on midnight-blue leather chairs in a room off the home clubhouse at Yankee Stadium. Some of Jeter's most important work is done in these rare rooms where cameras still don't venture. The space is important to Jeter because he knows he can't win by himself. His gift is getting others to buy into the group concept of winning. It's the Dwight D. Eisenhower view of leadership: not the simple execution of authority but, as the former president put it, "the art of getting someone else to do something that you want done because he wants to do it."

Getting a team to buy into everything it needs to do to win is what drives Jeter. This is apparent when I ask him what he will miss most about baseball. "Competing with your teammates," he says. "One of the biggest things about leadership is you have to get to know your teammates. You have to get to know who you're leading because there's different buttons you push with different people. Some guys you can yell and scream at, and some guys you have to put your arm around. You can do that only if you get to know them as people."

I remind Jeter about his reputation for how he treats teammates, media members, or associates who cross him. Jeter is said to draw a clear line when it comes to loyalty. Cross it once—dare to wrong him—and he coldly wants nothing more to do with the offender. You're off his team for good.

"Yeah, I've heard that about myself," he says. "But like what? You have to give me an example."

I bring up Chad Curtis, a former teammate. In 1999 the Yankees and the Mariners engaged in a nasty bench-clearing brawl. As players and coaches were being separated, Jeter and Alex Rodriguez, then with Seattle, were smiling and chatting with one another. Curtis engaged in an argument with Jeter in the dugout, then continued chastising him after the game in the clubhouse and in front of reporters. Four months later the Yankees traded Curtis to Texas for two minor leaguers.

"Now, see, don't even bring him up," Jeter says of Curtis, who last year was sentenced to seven to 15 years in prison for six counts of criminal sexual conduct. "I'm not going to throw stones when he's down. People think [about my reputation], Oh, there's one little incident and he's done with him. No. You may not know it because I choose not to speak about it, and if someone does something, they're not going to tell you about it. So there's more to stories."

So I try again. I mention Rodriguez. The two of them were close as young players. Then in 2001, Rodriguez took an unprovoked shot at Jeter in an *Esquire* story: "Jeter's been blessed with great talent all around him. He's never had to lead.... You go into New York, you wanna stop Bernie [Williams] and O'Neill. You never say, 'Don't let Derek beat you.' He's never your concern."

Rodriguez would later admit to using steroids at the time. He became Jeter's teammate in 2004; their relationship was cordial but lukewarm. Rodriguez was banned from baseball in Jeter's final season for his continued use of performance-enhancing drugs.

"Don't bring it up," Jeter says quietly, motioning to turn off the tape recorder. He has to go now. It's time to hit.

A Dodgers scout, Andy High, filed this report on the Yankees great in his last month:

"He can't stop quickly and throw hard. You can take the extra base on him…. He can't run and won't bunt…. His reflexes are very slow, and he can't pull a good fastball at all." Two months after the report ran in the Oct. 22, 1951, issue of *LIFE* magazine, Joe DiMaggio retired. DiMaggio hit .263 that season, 62 points below his career average. He was 36, complaining as he left how the introduction of night baseball took years off his career.

I ask Jeter what he will miss the least about baseball. "The schedule," he says. "I won't miss that. I mean, eight o'clock game tonight, we get into Tampa at four in the morning and we have to play another game? No, I won't miss that."

This year Jeter launched his own imprint with Simon & Schuster, Jeter Publishing. This week it released its first title, *The Contract*, an inspirational novel for young readers based on his childhood. He still wants to own a major league team someday. But, next year?

"That's the beauty of it. I don't know," he says. "You know what I want to do? Wake up one weekend and not have to go anywhere and do nothing.

"There are things I want to do in the future. But I think for me I need to get away for a while first. Come see me in eight months, and then maybe I can answer that question."

At the moment he is occupied with trying to scratch out a few hits. Ballplayers, even the greatest of them, make for lousy novelists: they write terrible endings. Ruth quit midseason in 1935 with a .181 average. Mickey Mantle was a .237 hitter on his way out in '68. Mike Schmidt, hitting .203, suddenly left in tears on an '89 road trip. Cal Ripken hit .239 in his exit year of 2001.

Jeter is no different, except for how much he has played this season: 139 games. Only four Hall of Famers ever played more in their last year: Jesse Burkett of the 1905 Red Sox (148),

Al Kaline of the '74 Tigers (147), George Brett of the '93 Royals (145), and Mantle (144). None of them hit better than .266.

The slow, painful death of a baseball career eventually fades from memory, as it did for the Mick and DiMag and the rest, and in our minds we keep them forever young. For Jeter, the apex of his youthful skills and his mastery in the spotlight was Oct. 26, 2000. It was the night the Yankees won a contentious, nerve-jangling, all-New York World Series against the Mets.

The Mets had seized momentum in the Series with a win in Game 3. Shortly before Jeter came to bat to begin Game 4, he smiled at Torre and said, "Don't worry, Mr. T, I got ya." Then he hit the first pitch of the game for a home run. The Yankees won 3–2. They were losing Game 5 in the sixth inning 2–1 when Jeter did it again, homering to tie the score. His postseason games were beginning to look as predictable as a *MacGyver* episode.

Jeter had become a regular of fall prime-time programming. October night after October night, there he was in the middle of a rally with the same twinkle in his eye he showed Torre, as if he had the advantage of having read the script ahead of time. It wasn't always that way. In his first postseason game, a loss against Texas in the 1996 ALDS, Jeter ended three innings with a total of six runners on before managing a hit his last time up. "Everyone wrote I was nervous and overmatched because I was a rookie," he says. "Too many people look at the result, and they want to make an issue of how someone is feeling inside. It just wasn't meant to be."

Torre still was learning about his rookie short-stop then. He wasn't sure if he needed to talk to the kid, settle him down. He kicked around the idea in his head until Jeter happened to walk past his office on his way out of the clubhouse that night. Jeter stuck his head into the doorway.

"Hey, Mr. T, make sure you get some sleep," Jeter said with that twinkle. "Tomorrow's the biggest game of your life."

"I always dreamed of playing in the major leagues. But everything that comes along with it couldn't have possibly been part of the dream. Because it's been much better."

Torre smiled and shook his head at the kid's confidence. The next night Jeter went 3-for-5, and the Yankees won 5–4. Beginning that night and up until the 2001 World Series, the Yankees won 76% of their postseason games (53–17) and 93% of their postseason series (14–1). Jeter batted .320 in that stretch.

Jeter is a career .310 hitter in the regular season and a .308 hitter in the postseason. He plays in the vein of Ernest Hemingway's answer when Dorothy Parker asked him, "Exactly what do you mean by guts?" Replied Hemingway, "I mean grace under pressure."

"I think part of that is focus," Jeter says. "So is work ethic. You do things over and over again, and when you get in a situation you like to think it comes natural. I think there has to be a mind-set that you're not afraid to fail. I'm not afraid to fail. I've done it quite a bit. The calmer you are, the more the game slows down for you, and I think part of that is controlling your emotions."

I go back to the night of Oct. 26, 2000, the apex. It wasn't just the home run, or that he had just become the first man to be named the MVP of the All-Star Game and the World Series in the same year. I walked out of the park with Jeter that night, exiting by way of the warning track in leftfield and out a gate in centerfield. Dressed in a slick, quicksilver suit with a silk white T-shirt beneath, he walked past New York City mayor Rudy Giuliani, who was playing catch in the

Yankees' bullpen, and Placido Domingo, who was in leftfield giddily shouting to Jeter that he had called his home run, and headed to a car to meet his date, Miss Universe, for a party at a Manhattan nightclub that would run until 5 a.m. in which people paid $12,000 to reserve a table in the inner sanctum near Jeter. He was 26 years old and already a four-time world champion. It was as dizzying as a Fellini movie, only real. Yet Jeter somehow stayed on balance. How could he do it?

That night at the club, trying to shout above the music and into his ear, I told Jeter that I needed to arrange an interview with him. He told me he would call me in two days: he was going out to dinner with his parents the day after tomorrow and would call me at 8 p.m., after they were done. While driving home that night I realized I had made a terrible mistake— he had my number, but I didn't have his. My entire story, which now would be up against its deadline, hinged on an athlete remembering to call me two days after saying he would in the wee hours at a Manhattan nightclub. I sweated out two days.

And then, precisely at 8 p.m. on the second night, my phone rang. It was Jeter: dinner with Mom and Dad was great; meet me at my apartment.

Who does that? Who wins the World Series MVP, dates Miss Universe, eats dinner with his parents, remembers to call a reporter, and—the first thing I noticed when I walked through his door was an ironing board, iron still at the ready—presses his own clothes? This is who: Dot and Charles' son.

Dot grew up as one of 14 children of a white church handyman in New Jersey. Charles, who is Black, was raised by his mother in Alabama and became a substance-abuse counselor. They never permitted Derek to use the word can't around the house. Anything was possible with hard work. There is no doubting whence comes his distaste for negativity.

"My parents are probably the most positive people you'll meet," Jeter says. "They're good to talk to, especially when you're struggling. They try to find something good that you've done. You could be 0-for-100, and it's, 'Oh, you'll get 'em tomorrow. You had some good swings.' And even though you may have been thinking, I did have some good swings, it feels good to hear someone say it."

Dot and Charles still go to many of their son's games. "It means a lot," Jeter says. "It's a comforting thing. It sounds funny saying that—I'm 40 years old now! They're not there all the time, but when they're there, I always know where they are."

It is beginning to come into focus. How many people influence a public life? "Oh, man, if I named them all, you'd have two pages just of names," he says. "You know, like the movie credits that roll at the end." But look back at the names he did bring up, and there is a theme. They all go back to before he became so familiar: Denbo, Butterfield, Williams, Raines, Torre.

Then I come across this: a former teammate, Matt Ruoff, this month telling *The Press Democrat* of Santa Rosa, Calif., "You always wanted to sit by him. I know that sounds weird. But Derek gave off a presence." Ruoff told a story about how Jeter went to the mound one time when one of the Yankees' pitchers was struggling and said, "You got nothing to lose. Stay with your changeup and

curve. Give me some ground balls. You're putting me to sleep out there."

Here's the kicker: these were the Gulf Coast League Yankees of 1992. The story could have been told by a teammate in 2014.

That's how you prosper across two decades in New York as the most familiar player there ever was: you were nearly fully formed before the klieg lights hit. The mortar of the man had set.

This season has been one long goodbye for Jeter. The Yankees threw a day for him on Sept. 7, when he thanked the fans for doing more for him than he did for them. "Did you see my hand shaking?" he says. "I was nervous. I get nervous quite a bit. I just hide it. I get butterflies before every game. It means you care."

It's not just the fans in New York. Every last stop for Jeter has brought an outpouring of thanks from fans.

"It's been surreal," Jeter says. "I'd be lying if I said it didn't feel good, because I guess they appreciate how you played. But more importantly, if you're an Orioles fan, a Rays fan, a Tigers fan, and you've been going to games over the last 20 years, whether they beat us or we beat them, there's a good chance that I was a part of it. And our job—we're playing a game—but our job is to entertain and bring joy to people, and I think people have appreciated it.

"I always dreamed of playing in the major leagues. But everything that comes along with it couldn't have possibly been part of the dream. Because it's been much better."

The last ovation will come on Sept. 28 at Fenway Park in Boston. All these people in all these cities are cheering not just a career with more base hits than all but five men who ever played the game. They also are cheering how he did it. And when they do, they also are cheering how Dot and Charles prepared him for the most brightly lit baseball life there ever was.

Here he stands, through two decades in Gotham, with integrity intact and hardly a scratch on him. •

Fans walk past a mural of Derek Jeter in the Bronx in 2018.

Excerpted from Sports Illustrated, February 7, 2018

The Boss Is Here

Inside Derek Jeter's quest to turn around the Marlins

BY TOM VERDUCCI

Cool as marble, choosing bemusement over anger, Derek Jeter is playing defense from behind a desk. It's a new position for the former Yankees shortstop. Start with the desk itself: a sleek, modern aircraft carrier with much of its vast deck gone unused. Jeter is behind it five days a week, usually starting, as on this one in January, around 7:45 a.m.

Room 2.18.06 of Marlins Park formerly belonged to David Samson, president of the Miami Marlins under owner Jeffrey Loria.

It featured dark walls and black carpeting. In a symbolic first act four months ago upon becoming a part-owner and chief executive officer of the franchise, Jeter turned the walls white and covered the floor with a light-beige Berber so luxurious that it requires a doormat at the entrance, lest any shoes dare track in dirt.

The bookshelves behind him contain only four items: one of his five Gold Glove Awards and three framed family photographs, including one of his daughter, Bella, now six months old, and a wedding shot with his wife, Hannah.

When Jeter announced his retirement as a player in 2014, players' association executive director Tony Clark said, "For nearly 20 years there has been no greater ambassador to the game of baseball than Derek Jeter." When Jeter turned 40 years old that summer, his number 2 Yankees jersey was not only still the top-selling jersey that season but also the most popular of all time.

That Derek Jeter is gone, at least if you read the blame assigned to him in a cascade of headlines out of Miami that portray what must be the worst honeymoon since Ernest Borgnine boarded the *SS Poseidon*. Jeter has been blamed for firing four "beloved" Marlins assistants, a scout who was in a hospital undergoing treatment for cancer, and the team's longtime play-by-play broadcaster; for bonus provisions tied to cutting payroll that can earn back his investment; for fronting an ownership group that needs money; for thinking he can boost attendance after trading his best players; for being irked he wasn't designated as the team's control person (i.e., the official top executive as recognized by Major League Baseball), and for blowing

off the winter meetings to yuk it up at a football game.

And that was just his first three months behind the desk.

The same guy who had been compared with icons Joe DiMaggio and Mickey Mantle is now being compared with malefactors Max Bialystock and Loria. He will address all of it. (One of the aforementioned charges against him, he admits, actually happens to be true.)

"You just don't turn into a new person because you're in a new position," Jeter says. "I don't treat people poorly. You would think some of these people covering the story might think, Well, you know what? That doesn't sound right. If you're a member of the media, you may say, look, I didn't give you a great quote. That's fine. But I don't treat people poorly. And you would think they would say, 'You know what? Let's at least reach out and see what he has to say.' But they've run with it. Like the gift-bag story. I addressed it publicly and it still lives on."

In 2011 the *New York Post* reported that Jeter gave gift baskets with signed memorabilia to women after they spent the night with him. Jeter denied it, but that did not stop many people from wanting it to be true. "It's the same thing here," he says. "So I don't know if me saying something even changes the narrative."

Few men in baseball ever amassed the portfolio of goodwill that Jeter did. He started a charitable organization, the Turn 2 Foundation, as a 22-year-old rookie. He is the greatest ballplayer to ever become a major league owner. He is the first Black CEO in baseball. A recent front office hire by the Marlins, upon meeting Jeter for the first time, says, "What was most apparent to me was how at ease and relaxed he is—a tremendous, relaxed confidence."

Like his friend and Marlins co-investor Michael Jordan, whose Charlotte Hornets have never won a playoff series in his 11 years as an NBA owner, Jeter knows he cannot answer his critics the same way he once could.

"When you're a player, you go out and have a good game, you silence the critics," says Jeter. "In this situation, the only way you silence your critics is over time.

"So if we're sitting here however many years down the road—I don't want to put a time frame on it—and we haven't been successful, then I think that would be fair criticism. But to criticize us before we even began and we're trying to fix something that, in my mind, has been broken— give us a little more time."

Jordan has a small stake in the Marlins of about $5 million. When Jeter turned to him for advice on being a CEO, Jordan told him, "If you believe in the plan, stick to the plan. Don't alter it midstream."

"And that," Jeter says, "is exactly what we're going to do."

What is that plan? On the business side Jeter is reaching out to the community in ways Loria never did. He is turning Marlins Park into an entertainment venue beyond the Marlins' 81 home dates. (Monster truck rallies and craft beer festivals are already scheduled.) He will explore selling naming rights to the ballpark. He hopes to attract more fans with music and a festival atmosphere at ball games, similar to what was seen during the World Baseball Classic last year. ("Eighty-five percent of those fans were from the Miami area. Those fans are here," he says.) And he hopes to more than double the worst local TV deal in the game ($20 million a year on a contract that expires in 2020).

On the baseball side he wants a team that plays "the right way," looks professional ("Well-groomed is the best way to put it," he says when asked about a facial hair policy), and, from the lowest level of the minors to the majors, emphasizes winning—all of which more than suggests a team in his image. Jeter has known only the Yankees and their demanding, win-centric system. "There's a way that you work," he says. "There's a way that you're accountable. I never want to be the person who says, 'Well, when I played…' But when we were coming up we knew there was a way to handle yourself. That's something that needs to be instilled in players when they first sign.

"The bottom line is we're here to win, and anybody here should have that mind-set. And if you're not on the same page? Then this won't be the place for you."

The Marlins are not the Yankees. Not even close. They haven't made the playoffs in 14 seasons and have had eight straight losing years. The team is saddled with $400 million in debt. The farm system Jeter inherited was one of the worst in baseball. The team has finished last in NL attendance in 12 of the past 13 seasons. It has lost more than 600,000 paid customers since Marlins Park opened in 2012. The fan base is distrustful after the spend-and-slash ways of previous owners Wayne Huizenga and Loria, not to mention how Loria and MLB squeezed Miami-Dade County and the city of Miami to help build Marlins Park with what will turn out to be about $2 billion in bonds in one of the most lopsided public financing deals in sports.

Into this mess rides Jeter, who has never run a team before, who never liked watching baseball on television as a player, and who on the final day of last season at Marlins Park watched his first game from the stands since he went to Tiger Stadium as a high schooler. What makes him think this can work?

Those who ask that question simply don't know Jeter. He will run the Marlins with the same diligence, purpose, and confidence he wielded as a player. Jordan need not worry about Jeter sticking to the plan. In 1992, after being drafted in the first round out of Central High in Kalamazoo, Jeter reported to the Yankees' minor league facility and, for the first time, needed a wood bat. He scoured the forest of bats in storage bins until he found one that most resembled the shape of the metal bat he used in high school. He would use the same model bat for every one of his 3,465 hits, sixth-most

all time. He used the same closed-web glove his entire career.

His first pro manager, with the 1992 Gulf Coast Yankees, was Gary Denbo, who would later become his hitting coach, the guru who helped build the Yankees' minor league system into one of baseball's best, and the first man Jeter hired in Miami. Denbo is the Marlins' vice president of player development and scouting.

"I've learned over the years," Denbo says, "that once he sets his mind to something he usually gets it done. Same as he did as a player, he's putting in the work. He's putting in the hours."

———————

Let's start with the money. Last August, Loria selected a bid from a group led by Bruce Sherman—with Jeter on board—as the one he would present to MLB's ownership committee as the winning offer to buy the Marlins. In 1986 Sherman cofounded the money management firm Private Capital Management, which he sold in 2001 for about $1.3 billion. The price tag for the Marlins: $1.2 billion. Sherman's group would write a check for $790.5 million, with Sherman footing almost half the tab, and assume the team's $400 million in debt.

Jeter made it known that he wanted to be the Marlins' control person. As the deal neared the finish line, Samson told him that designation would not be possible. Jeter did not have a large enough stake in the equity of the team. (Reports have pegged Jeter's investment at $25 million.)

"I keep hearing about my 'modest' investment," Jeter says. "I wish that were the case. One, it's not small. And two, that's not accurate, no."

According to a source familiar with the deal, Jeter is the sixth-largest stakeholder in the Marlins, contributing slightly less than 5% of the equity, or $37.9 million. Asked to confirm that number, Jeter says, "Oh, it went up? Before it was 25. It's higher than 25."

Samson knew that members of the powerful ownership committee, all of whom hold large

During batting practice with
Marlins players in 2019.

stakes in their respective clubs, were not likely to approve "someone with a smaller stake and who didn't have any [ownership] experience," an MLB source said. So the bid went to the ownership committee with Sherman listed as the control person. The sale was unanimously approved on Sept. 27. According to Denbo, Jeter dreamed of becoming a major league owner "at least 10 years ago. We'd be working in the batting cage and he would say that he wouldn't be a coach or a manager but he had aspirations to buy a team." Asked if he were disappointed not to be the control person, Jeter admits, "Of course. Of course."

In August the Sherman-Jeter group prepared a prospective for potential investors dubbed Project Wolverine (after the mascot of the University of Michigan, which Jeter attended for one semester after the 1992 season). Five months later the *Miami Herald* revealed details from the document after two potential investors shared it with the newspaper.

According to the *Herald*, Project Wolverine projected the Marlins to cut payroll in 2018 from $115 million to $90 million, but forecasts a 25% gain in ticket revenue and a 19% gain in attendance. Corporate sponsorship would almost double in three years, the prospective claimed. In addition, Jeter could help recoup his "modest financial investment," the *Herald* said, through a $5 million salary and a series of bonuses tied to team profitability, prompting Joel Sherman of the *New York Post* to equate Jeter with Bialystock, the fictional character from *The Producers* who makes money with an intentionally inferior product.

"They were trying to raise money," an MLB executive source says about the optimism of Project Wolverine. "You can't show a plan that's going to bleed money for seven years. Who's going to invest in a plan like that?"

Says Jeter, "The model you have is an old model. A lot of times you put together models and assumptions before you really get here and get under the hood. So things change once you really get a look at what's going on.

"I'm not saying we don't have lofty goals. People are so focused on the model from August. It's changed. We've found out quite a bit since we got in here."

Jeter has traded every bit of what was one of the best young outfields in baseball—Giancarlo Stanton, 28; Marcell Ozuna, 27; and Christian Yelich, 26—as well as second baseman Dee Gordon, 29. The moves saved the team roughly $40 million on the 2018 payroll.

A $5 million salary for a CEO, according to the MLB executive, "is in the high range, but for a CEO that has a stake in the team maybe not unheard of."

Says Jeter, "The speculation of what they say my salary is—$5 million?—that's not true. And then I get a bonus based on what?"

Profitability.

"Not true," he says. "That's not true."

Jeter, dressed in a crisp blue suit and white shirt open at the neck, is standing in the dugout of Marlins Park, which is dramatically lit for "Dinner on the Diamond," a January function for about 150 potential business partners, sponsors, and season ticket holders. They dine on tables arranged across the infield. A 12-piece band at home plate plays Latin music. The roof of Marlins Park, a modern, stylish ballpark that fits the South Florida aesthetic, is cracked just enough to reveal a swath of stars. Jeter, as DiMaggio did, evokes a casual elegance and commands any space he enters, even one this big. He is here to schmooze and sell. Before the dinner he glided from conversation to conversation in a cocktail hour in a private club.

"The old ownership didn't do anything like this," says one of the guests, Ivan Herrera, CEO of UniVista Insurance in Miami. "New ownership is reaching out to the community. It's time for a change, and [Jeter] realizes that. I think he's doing the right thing. He's got my support."

In the dugout, Jeter is reviewing his notes for his dinner talk when his phone stirs with a text. It's from Joe Torre, chief baseball officer for MLB and Jeter's manager for 12 years with the Yankees.

"Uh-oh, it's Mr. T," Jeter says. "I still get nervous when I know it's him. It's like, 'What did I do? Is there a fine I still haven't paid?'"

Like Denbo, former teammates Jorge Posada and Gerald Williams, former agent Casey Close, and selected others, Torre is part of Jeter's small but fiercely tight inner circle of confidantes. Jeter harbors no quarter for gossipers and negativists, and his circle of trust reflects like-minded loyalists he has known for many years. (Denbo, for instance, gave this Jeterian answer when asked for his reaction to the avalanche of criticism toward Jeter: "I can't give you a reaction. I don't read the paper. I've learned over the years in New York to stay away from negative media.")

Jeter is bound to quote Torre on baseball matters, such as on the use of advanced analytics. "This organization is way behind in the analytics department, so that's something we're focusing on," Jeter says. "But I think there is a human element. Mr. T says it perfectly: players have heartbeats. Analytics are great, but you still have to take the time to know the player. So there's a hybrid in there.

"If I had time I'd go to Analytics 101. I've got to brush up on my Spanish. I understand a little more than I speak. Would I take classes? No question, I would."

It's time for Jeter to sell. He walks out of the dugout, crosses the third-base line, and waits, perfectly enough, at shortstop. Jeter played his last game on Sept. 28, 2014. That was the last time he picked up a bat—or even thought about playing baseball.

"When I retired people would say, 'Oh, wait till spring training comes around. You're going to miss it,'" Jeter says. "I can honestly say there has not been one day where I missed playing. And that's a good thing. I got everything out of my system, and there's nothing left."

Then the man who played in more postseason games than any ballplayer ever, with more runs, singles, doubles, triples, and total bases, and who won five World Series, catches himself.

"If I could wake up and play in the playoffs, maybe. But I don't miss it, no. In my mind that was it. It was like a switch. I turned the light off."

He walks to the podium with that unmistakable gait—slightly bow-legged and as erect as if wearing a crown. He has notes in front of him to remind him of the topics he wants to address, but he otherwise wings it superbly. He promises season ticket holders are part of "an exclusive club, and you will be treated accordingly." He tells potential sponsors that "Marlins Park is open for business. It is an entertainment venue and it should be used for more than just baseball." He says the backbone of success is building a strong farm system. "This is a new day," he tells them. "We are sticking with our plan… There will be no excuses tolerated. We will become the team you deserve."

Jeter does not eat at Dinner on the Diamond, because he eats at home with his wife and daughter whenever he can. He goes to bed early and gets up early; don't expect him to be watching other teams' late-night games. "Yeah," he says with a laugh about such an idea, "let me come here all day long and then go home and watch other games. See how that works out. As serious and as big as things seem here, the number one priority is your family."

After the event he drives the 15 minutes to his residence in Coconut Grove, a 5,200-square foot, 19th-floor apartment he is renting. Later that night, as he is getting ready for bed, his phone buzzes with a message from Jason Latimer, his VP of communications and outreach. It includes a link to a story that just broke about Yelich's agent lobbying for a trade. Jeter puts the phone down without opening the link and goes to bed.

"I try when I get home to stay off my phone after certain hours," he says.

He does not open the link until the next morning, and only after he cuddles with his daughter.

"My wife and I race in there in the morning to see who can get there first when she starts crying a little bit and then starts smiling," says Jeter. "It's the best part of the day.

"I love being a dad. Absolutely love it. Puts things in perspective. She doesn't talk yet, but when you get home and somebody's happy to see you, regardless of what happened, it makes your day."

At the end of last season, with the Sherman-Jeter group only days into taking ownership of the Marlins, the team's best player, Stanton, sat down with president of baseball operations Michael Hill and told him he wanted out if the team was going to go through a rebuild.

(On Jeter's orders, the word *rebuild* is verboten among employees; he prefers to call it a "build.")

"When we got the team our thought was that he was going to be a part of it moving forward," says Jeter, though that would have meant one player eating up 30% of the payroll. "He has a no-trade clause. The plan was he's on our team."

Stanton had played eight seasons in Miami, all of them losing seasons, and he wanted to stay only if this ownership group was going to spend money to fortify the pitching staff. Thanks to their core of young hitters, the 2017 Marlins ranked fifth in the NL in runs. But their pitching was abysmal. Only two teams in the league gave up more runs.

"When we were at the town hall," says Jeter, referring to an event when he took questions from season ticket holders last December, "one of the fans said, 'All you needed to do was sign two pitchers.' I said, 'Okay, who are those two pitchers?' He couldn't answer. You could have added two pitchers to this team and they still wouldn't have won."

Jake Arrieta and Yu Darvish, the top free agent pitchers?

"No," Jeter says. "They still wouldn't have won. So you just dig a bigger hole, and eventually you have to get out of it. That's a lot of work."

Seeing the writing on the wall, Stanton gave Hill a list of four teams to which he would accept a trade: the Dodgers, Cubs, Astros, and Yankees. Hill called each of the four teams about Stanton. None showed interest. The Dodgers told Hill they had debt service issues and "couldn't make the money work." The Cubs told him they were squirreling away money to pay their core of young hitters. The Astros were satisfied with their outfield and DH depth. The Yankees had their eye on Japanese free agent pitcher/outfielder Shohei Ohtani.

"So I expanded the pool," Hill says. "I talked to all 29 clubs. We got traction with St. Louis and San Francisco."

Stanton agreed to meet with the Giants on Nov. 30 and Cardinals the next day in California, and then flew to Miami. He sat down with the Marlins executives on the morning of Dec. 5. It was the first time Jeter spoke with Stanton about trade scenarios.

"These are the only two clubs," Hill told Stanton. "It's in your hands."

Says Hill, "It was written that we threatened him. How can you threaten a guy with a no-trade clause?"

Three days later, Stanton confirmed that he would not accept a trade to the Giants or Cardinals. On the same day, a repeat call by Hill to the Yankees proved fruitful. What changed? Five days earlier New York learned that Ohtani had ruled them out as a potential destination.

Yankees GM Brian Cashman told Hill he would include Jacoby Ellsbury in a deal for Stanton. Hill told him no, the Marlins wanted no part of a declining player with $68 million due him over the next three seasons. The two men quickly hung up.

A short while later Cashman called back. He made another offer, substituting second baseman Starlin Castro (due $22 million over the next two years) for Ellsbury.

"When Castro was in," Hill says, "then you knew a deal was a possibility."

Denbo and Dan Greenlee, the Marlins' new director of player personnel, spent all night and the next morning digging through the Yankees' system to determine which prospects they wanted. Hill wanted the Yankees to take the entire $295 million remaining on Stanton's contract—"You don't want to send any money when you're trading the reigning MVP," he says—but he knew that "to get better quality players in return," he would have to kick in cash. The Marlins included $30 million in the deal, getting back prospects Jorge Guzman, 22, a pitcher, and José Devers, 18, an infielder—a take that critics considered too light, driven more by finances than by talent.

"Anyone who makes that comment doesn't understand what we do as general managers," Hill says. "More than ever, there are so many smart people working in other front offices. They all have parameters to work with. A 10-year commitment and $295 million, you're not talking about 29 clubs with the ability to take that contract. Anybody who says we didn't get enough obviously never sat in this chair."

The critics took shots at Jeter, too. Why didn't he talk more with Stanton? Why shop him to teams not on his preferred list?

"I'm the president of baseball operations," Hill says. "That's not [Jeter's] job. Unfounded and unfair. He's the CEO. He's got to get his arms around so many things in addition to baseball. [Trade talks], that's my job. I bounced everything by him."

Two days later, as the winter meetings began in Orlando, Jeter was seen in a luxury box watching the Dolphins play on *Monday Night Football*. Wrote David Hyde of the *Sun-Sentinel*, "The Marlins burn. He watches the Dolphins. The baseball world laughs at this franchise. He sits among The Beautiful People."

"It's just a bad look," says a rival GM. "I know he's the CEO. But it would be better if like the rest of us he's at the whiteboard in the [winter meetings] suite at 2 a.m. grinding it out, studying roster spots and how the team can get better."

Jeter says he never planned to attend the winter meetings because that responsibility falls to Hill. Moreover, he attended the Dolphins game through an invitation to meet with local business leaders about possible partnerships. But by then, Jeter's doorstep had become a dumping ground of criticism. He took heat for the departures of Jack McKeon, Jeff Conine, and Andre Dawson, who had served as advisers to Samson.

"They are no longer special assistants to David Samson," Jeter explains. "He's no longer here. In my mind, that's simple."

Jeter did offer the advisers a reduced role at a significant pay cut. None accepted. Jeter told fans at his town hall, "Those individuals were treated appropriately and with respect."

Jeter also took heat for the removal of play-by-play broadcaster Rich Waltz, even though Fox Sports, the local rights-holder for Marlins games, said publicly that the decision was theirs alone. Jeter did not know Waltz, nor had he seen his work.

Nothing created as much negativity for Jeter, however, than the dismissal of a Marlins scout, Marty Scott, who was recovering from colon cancer treatment. Scott, 64, told Yahoo! Sports he was "very hurt" to learn with two weeks left on his contract that he wasn't coming back, saying, "If I knew I was going to fire somebody, I did it at the beginning of September."

The Sherman-Jeter group did not gain operational control of the team until Oct. 2. Most standard employee contracts in baseball expire on Oct. 31. In the second week of October the baseball operations department began the process of reviewing which of the Loria-Samson hires would be renewed. Scott's review was put on hold because of his hospitalization.

"We were incredibly sensitive to what Marty was going through," Hill says. "We were trying to allow him to go through what he was going through. Marty wanted to know and kept calling to try to get an answer."

Only upon the inquiries from Scott, Hill says, did pro scouting director Jim Cuthbert inform Scott his contract would not be renewed. "Our desire is to be a first-class organization and treat people with respect," Hill says. "How it was portrayed was not entirely accurate…Our CEO has nothing to do with it. We make our evaluations departmentally and we take them up the chain of command in terms of changes we'd like to make."

Says Jeter about Scott's dismissal, "The scout, I don't even want to get into. He has health issues. There's no reason to go down that path."

Wrote Greg Cote of the *Miami Herald* of Jeter, "To call those moves callous is bad enough. To call them Loriaesque may be an even greater indictment." *The Atlantic* piled on last month, writing, "Few athletes have entered a front-office role with as spotless a reputation, and fewer athletes have compromised that reputation so quickly."

Jeter owns a 32,000-square-foot waterfront mansion in Tampa. It has become a white elephant. He originally planned to return to Tampa on weekends, but in his first four months as Marlins CEO he spent just five days there: two at Thanksgiving and three at Christmas.

The Yankees won 60% of the games in which Jeter played. "Winning is the best," he says. "Winning a championship. That's why you put all the work in. And that mind-set doesn't change now in this position."

"I'm here," he says. "You have to be here."

Like all employees, he wears a photo identification badge, which is attached to his belt. He taps into the coffee machine outside his office all day long. "I'm turning into my dad," he says as he draws yet another cup, this from someone who never drank coffee until his last few years as a player, and then only one cup before a game. He has just come from one of his frequent breakfasts with prospective investors and sponsors. Almost immediately after the Sherman-Jeter group purchased the team, the Marlins' owners cast lines among wealthy local businesspeople for more money, this time with a prospective called Project Citrus. The effort was read widely as a signal that the ownership group was underfunded.

"Bruce Sherman is very wealthy," says a senior MLB executive. "We don't have any concern about their financial wherewithal. It's actually a very well-financed group."

Says Jeter, "The equity check that was struck for this team was the largest equity check that was struck for any team in the history of the game." The MLB executive confirmed that claim.

"People thinking that we are out there raising money because we are broke, that is not the case," Jeter says. "One thing we wanted was to have local people in Miami invested in the team—to add to our group. It makes us stronger as an organization. Having said that, if we don't raise another dime—hey, we've got a lot of money. Don't think that we don't."

In front of Jeter's desk is an enormous aquarium filled with colorful fish, and a conference table on the other side. To his left are floor-to-ceiling windows, dappled with the shadows of palm trees that sway in the trade winds that carry over South Beach and Biscayne Bay. This morning is the kind of brilliant that forces a Northerner, unbound from winter's long twilight, to squint.

If you summon the prime version of Jeter in your mind's eye, up pops either that marionette-like, inside-out swing carving a humble single to rightfield or, most of all, the quick fist pump after a win, the equivalent imprimatur of Nike, the goddess of victory, raising the victor's garland.

The Yankees won 60% of the games in which Jeter played. "Winning is the best," he says. "Winning a championship. That's why you put all the work in. And that mind-set doesn't change now in this position."

Pressure never shook him. Jeter hit .310 in the regular season and .308 in the postseason. Now that equanimity—the marble in him, with its high compressive strength—is tested again, but in the worst market in the league, with the worst TV contract, with $400 million of debt, a roster stripped of its best players, and a name and a title so big as to bear every bit of blame. He made $265 million as a player. He doesn't need this. Or does he?

"Why?" he says, repeating an inquiry about why he is behind this desk. "It's always been a dream. I want to build something and be proud of it. It's going to be a challenge here. But you've got to like challenges. If it were easy it wouldn't be worth it.

"We believe we can turn this thing around. A lot of people viewed [the optimism] as a negative, or viewed it as us being crazy. But I think it's a good thing. Correct me if I'm wrong, but the fan base should be happy that you have an ownership group that believes the fan base is coming back to the stadium. I will never apologize for believing in the Miami market."

In the cocktail hour before the Dinner on the Diamond event, grown-ups swooned around Jeter, posing for pictures and asking him to sign Yankees jerseys. He is the face of the Marlins, for better, as on nights like this, or for worse.

Ralph Eguilior, an architect from Miami, walked up to Jeter. "I hope you're as good an owner as you were a shortstop," he said.

Jeter smiled and said, "Better." •

2021 WO
BAS
CLA

WorldBaseballCl

2021
WORLD

THE COVERS

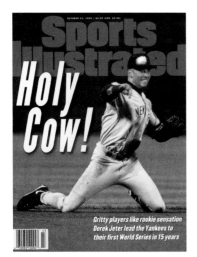

Oct. 21, 1996

June 21, 1999

June 7, 2004

Feb. 24, 1997

Oct. 23, 2000

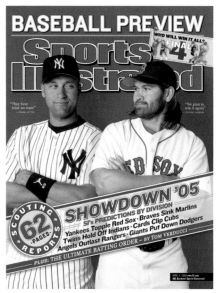

April 4, 2005

May 18, 1998

Oct. 22, 2001

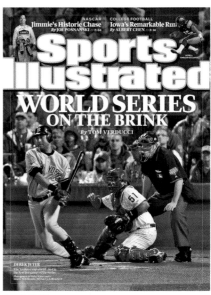

Nov. 9, 2009

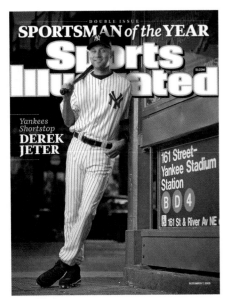

Dec. 7, 2009

May 3, 2010

Sept. 29, 2014

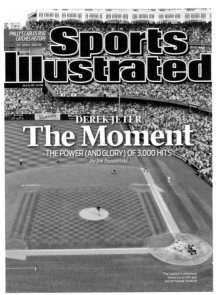

July 18, 2011

Photo Credits

Al Tielemans: Pages 60-61; Chuck Solomon: Pages 58-59, 78-79, 88-89, 95-96, 102-03, 106-07; Damian Strohmeyer: Pages 104-05, 128-29, 132-33, 152-53; Erick Rasco: Pages 120, 162-63, 166-67, 178-79, 216-17; Heinz Kluetmeier: Pages 20-21, 86-87, 93; John Biever: Pages 54-55, 136-37, 164-65, 191; John Iacono: Pages 5-6, 17, 18, 34-35, 63, 80, 81, 108-09; Robert Beck: Pages 74-75, 82-83, 114-15, 130-31, 138-39, 154-55; Simon Bruty: Pages 111, 175, 176, 232, 148-49, 150-51, 168-69, 170-71, 172-73, 180-81, 182-83; V.J. Lovero: Pages 48-49, 56-57, 76-77, 84-85; Walter Iooss Jr.: Pages 1, 2, 4-5, 25, 29, 30, 46-47, 50-51, 68-69, 100-01, 134-35, 145

Additional photography: Al Bello/Getty Images: Pages 146, 197, 213, 184-85, 204-05; Anthony J. Causi/Icon Sportswire via Getty Images: Page 125; Doug Pensinger/Allsport: Pages 36-37; Eric Espada/Getty Images: Pages 228-29; Ezra Shaw/Getty Images: Pages 98-99; Focus On Sport/Getty Images: Pages 8, 9, 11, 15, 16, 126-27; Jamie Squire/Getty Images: Page 53; Jeff Kravitz/FilmMagic Inc.: Page 31; Jim McIsaac/Getty Images: Pages 195, 199, 200-01, 202-03; John G. Mabanglo/AFP via Getty Images: Page 72; Michael Heiman/Getty Images: Pages 159, 160-61; Michael Reaves/Getty Images: Page 222; Mike Ehrmann/Getty Images: Page 219; Rich Pilling/MLB via Getty Images: Pages 22-23, 32-33; Ron Tringali/MLB via Getty Images: Pages 187, 192-93; Ron Vesely/Getty Images: Page 71; Ted Mathias/AFP via Getty Images: Page 19

This book is available in quantity at special discounts for your group or organization. For further information, contact:

Triumph Books LLC
814 North Franklin Street
Chicago, Illinois 60610
(312) 337-0747
www.triumphbooks.com

Printed in U.S.A.
ISBN: 978-1-62937-948-7

Number 2,
Derek Jeter.